ANI DiFRANCO

ANI DiFRANCO

Righteous Babe

Raffaele Quirino

QUARRY
MUSIC
BOOKS

Dedicated to the most important and
wonderful women in my life: Lynda,
Elyse Christine, and Arden Yvonne Quirino.

The publisher gratefully acknowledges the
support of The Canada Council for the Arts
and the Book Publishing Industry Development Program
of the Department of Canadian Heritage.

Ani DiFranco: Righteous Babe is a serious critical and biographical study of the music and
career of Ani DiFranco. The quotation of lyrics from songs written or performed by
Ani DiFranco illustrates the biographical and critical information and analysis presented
by the author and thus constitutes fair use under existing copyright conventions.
All Ani DiFranco lyrics copyright by Righteous Babe Music/BMI.

ISBN 1-55082-253-5

Design by Susan Hannah.
Typeset by Robert Stewart.
Cover and color insert photographs by Sean Powers.

Printed and bound in Canada by AGMV Marquis,
Cap-Saint-Ignace, Quebec.

Published by Quarry Press Inc.,
PO Box 1061,
Kingston, Ontario,
K7L 4Y5 Canada.

www.quarrypress.com.

THE CANADA COUNCIL   LE CONSEIL DES ARTS
FOR THE ARTS   DU CANADA

CONTENTS

Logo from Righteous Babe Records catalog.

Songwriter,
Musicmaker,
Storyteller, Freak

AN OPEN LETTER FROM ANI DIFRANCO TO MS MAGAZINE…

November 5, 1997

Marcia Ann Gillespie
Editor in Chief
Ms. Magazine
135 W. 50th Street
16 Floor
New York, NY 10020

So I'm poring through the 25th anniversary issue of Ms.
(on some airplane going somewhere in the amorphous blur that
amounts to my life) and I'm finding it endlessly enlightening
and stimulating as always, when, whaddaya know, I come across
a little picture of little me. I was flattered to be included in that
issue's "21 feminists for the 21st century" thingybob. I think

ya'll are runnin' the most bold and babeolishious magazine around, after all.

Problem is, I couldn't help but be a little weirded out by the paragraph next to my head that summed up her me-ness and my relationship to the feminist continuum. What got me was that it largely detailed my financial successes and sales statistics. My achievements were represented by the fact that I "make more money per album sold than Hootie and the Blowfish," and that my catalogue sales exceed 3/4 of a million. It was specified that I don't just have my own record company but my own "profitable" record company. Still, the ironic conclusion of the aforementioned blurb is a quote from me insisting "it's not about the money." Why then, I ask myself, must "the money" be the focus of so much of the media that surrounds me? Why can't I escape it, even in the hallowed halls of Ms.?

Firstly, the "Hootie and the Blowfish" business was not my doing. The L.A. Times financial section wrote an article about my record label, Righteous Babe Records, in which they raved about the business savvy of a singer (me) who thwarted the corporate overhead by choosing to remain independent, thereby pocketing $4.25 per unit, as opposed to the $1.25 made by Hootie or the $2 made by Michael Jackson. This story was then picked up and reprinted by The New York Times, Forbes, the Financial News Network and (lo and behold) Ms.

So, here I am, publicly morphing into some kinda Fortune 500-young-entrepreneur-from-hell, and all along I thought I was just a folksinger!

OK, it's true. I do make a much larger profit (percentage-wise) than the Hootster. What's even more astounding is that there are thousands of musicians out there who make an even higher profit percentage than me! How many local musicians are there in your community who play gigs in bars and coffee shops about town? I bet lots of them have made cassettes or CDs that they'll happily sell to you with a personal smile from the edge of the stage or back at the bar after their set. Would you believe these shrewd, profit-minded wheeler-dealers are pocketing a whopping 100% of the profits on the sales of those puppies?! Wait till the Financial News Network gets a whiff of them!

I sell approximately 2.5% of the albums that a Joan Jewelanis Morrisette sells and get about 0.5% of the airplay royalties, so obviously if it all comes down to dollars and cents, I've led a wholly unremarkable life. Yet I choose relative statistical mediocrity over fame and fortune because I have a bigger purpose in mind. Imagine how strange it must be for a girl who has spent 10 years fighting as hard as she could against the lure of the corporate carrot and the almighty forces of capital, only to be eventually recognized by the power structure as a business pioneer.

I have indeed sold enough records to open a small office on a half-abandoned main street in the dilapidated urban center of my home town, Buffalo, N.Y. I am able to hire 15 or so folks to run and constantly reinvent the place while I drive around and play music for people. I am able to give stimulating business to local printers and manufacturers and to employ the services of independent distributors, promoters, booking agents and publicists. I was able to quit my day job and devote myself to what I love.

And yes, we are enjoying modest profits these days, affording us the opportunity to reinvest in innumerable political and artistic endeavors. RBR is no Warner Bros. But it is a going concern, and for me, it is a vehicle for redefining the relationship between art and commerce in my own life. It is a record company that is the product not just of my own imagination, but that of my friend and manager Scot Fisher and of all the people who work there. People who incorporate and coordinate politics, art and media every day into a people-friendly, sub-corporate, woman-informed, queer-happy small business that puts music before rock stardom and ideology before profit.

And me. I'm just a folksinger, not an entrepreneur. My hope is that my music and poetry will be enjoyable and/or meaningful to someone, somewhere, not that I maximize my profit margins. It was 15 years and 11 albums getting to this place of notoriety and, if anything, I think I was happier way back when. Not that I regret any of my decisions, mind you. I'm glad I didn't sign on to the corporate army. I mourn the commodification and homogenization of music by the music industry, and I fear the manufacture of consent by the corporately-controlled media. Last thing I want to do is feed the machine.

I was recently mortified while waiting in the dressing room before one of my shows. Some putz suddenly takes the stage to announce me and exclaim excitedly that this was my "largest sold-out crowd to date!" "Oh, really," I'm thinking to myself, "that's interesting . . . too bad it's not the point." All of my achievements are artistic, as are all of my failures.

I have so much respect for Ms. magazine. If I couldn't pick it up at newsstands my brain probably would've atrophied by now on some trans-Atlantic flight and I would be lying limp and twitchy in a bed of constant travel, staring blankly into the abyss of the gossip magazines. Ms. is a structure of media wherein women are able to define themselves, and articulate for themselves those definitions. We wouldn't point to 21 of the feminists moving into the 21st century and define them in terms of "Here's Becky Ballbuster from Iowa City, she's got a great ass and a cute little button nose . . . " No ma'am. We've gone beyond the limited perceptions of sexism and so we should move beyond the language and perspective of the corporate patriarchy. The Financial News Network may be ultimately impressed with me now that I've proven to them that there's a life beyond the auspices of papa Sony, but do I really have to prove this to you?

We have the ability and the opportunity to recognize women

not just for the financial successes of their work but for the work itself. we have the facility to judge each other by entirely different criteria than those imposed upon us by the superstructure of society. we have a view that reaches beyond profit margins into poetry, and a vocabulary to articulate the difference.

Thanks for including me Ms., really. But just promise me one thing; if I drop dead tomorrow, tell me my grave stone won't read:

ani d.
CEO.

Please let it read:

songwriter
musicmaker
storyteller
freak.

Ani DiFranco

THE SOUND OF RIGHTEOUSNESS

No matter how hard you try, you can't get into Ani DiFranco's mind. Believe me, I've tried. It isn't easy to get a hold on someone who has such a headstrong passion for life, love, happiness, anger, and righteousness. Seemingly at once everywoman and heroine, straight and lesbian, subculture rebel and pop culture diva, antistar and megastar. Somewhat daunted, I started reading everything I could: magazine articles, newspaper stories, rock music guide reviews and listings. I spent hours on the Internet reading articles, looking through news groups, entertainment websites and just plain junk. I spoke with her publicist, wrote to her manager, read the press kits, and more. Short of setting up camp outside her home in Buffalo, I tried to get into Ani's mind. No luck. What I realized is that her mind operates on many different, wonderful levels, simultaneously, it seems. A hard thing to grasp. But the more I read about her, the more I thought she was someone I could, at the very least, admire. I admired her sense of ethics, her passion for life, and zest for discovery. Her undaunted search for the truth and love, justice and compassion.

The closest I could come to getting inside Ani's mind was getting inside her music. I listened to her recordings, time after time, with my music critic's ear. Then I read the lyrics over and over and over. Out loud and in the silence of my own synapses. Her recordings reach me the way I like to be reached — with superb word-play, intense music-making, unique creativity. My other musical heroes, like Tom Robinson, Richard Thompson, Beth Orton, Guy Clark, Luka Bloom, and Lloyd Cole (among others), all share these characteristics. Ani has these qualities in spades. It's the voice of pure thought and poetry combining to reveal truths and passions, thoughts and frustrations, anxieties and happiness.

And so this book is inspired in part by my admiration for Ani DiFranco the outspoken voice of her generation, a woman of ideas and beliefs, a feminist, a DIY (Do It Yourself) pioneer, a self-reliant business woman, a freak. But this book is also a record of how Ani DiFranco's music has inspired me — and thus the large section devoted to my evaluation of her music and lyrics album by album, song by song. This is a book about Ani DiFranco's music, foremost — about Ani DiFranco songwriter, musicmaker, storyteller — and about her life and career, only by the way of trying to understand the source and context for her music. This book is about the Ani DiFranco experience. It isn't Ani's story. Only Ani can write that story. This is my interpretation of Ani's story seen through the events which have marked her life (so far), through some of the things she's been quoted as saying, through the way she's perceived by her fans, and especially through her recordings.

My first introduction to Ani (and it is pronounced Ah-nee) DiFranco came when I stumbled across a used copy of LITTLE PLASTIC CASTLE at Ollie's CDs in Newmarket (thanks Peter!). My four-year-old, Elyse, was with me at the time. The moment I picked up the disc, Elyse looked at its bright aquamarine cover and said, "Can we get this one, Daddy?"

"Why, Elyse?"

"It has a mermaid on it."

And sure enough, it looked like it did. On the body of a large goldfish appeared Ani DiFranco's head. My daughter, then a "so-much-more-intelligent-than-three" kid with an old soul, had a thing for mermaids.

I bought the disc for two reasons. Elyse was the first. The second had more to do with the fact that I had never heard a single Ani DiFranco note, lyric or lick. I didn't know what she sounded like, whether I'd like it, or hate it. I had assumed (never assume!) that she was yet another in a long line of "angst-in-pants" femme rockers rendered "famous" after the sales fallout generated by Alanis Morissette's JAGGED LITTLE PILL. I knew she had achieved a fair amount of success by recording her type of music on her own record label. I mistook her for someone who appeared *after* Alanis's big album hit the peak of the charts. I was wrong.

I chastise myself when I dismiss things so casually. I take it upon myself to prove I'm right (or wrong!) based on first-hand experience. So I plunked down the cash and plunged into Ani's world. Fortunately, the trip was worth it. I found LITTLE PLASTIC CASTLE to be a thought-provoking, intense, fully-realized work of incredible maturity by a songwriter in peak form.

And it got me thinking: How did she do it? How did she accomplish the task of becoming a self-made artist in this day and age of mass media, socio-cultural hogwash, and flavor-of-the-month music-making? Here was a tough woman. Wrote and performed her own songs at an early age, started her own company selling records out of her car trunk while gigging up and down the continent. Was courted by minor and major record companies alike yet refused to compromise herself by signing to anyone. Kept total control over her music, her album covers, t-shirt/merchandise sales, her own image f'chrissakes. Kept it with her at all times, never gave it up, not one iota to anyone at all, ever.

One of the things I began to wonder about when I sat down and listened to every note she ever sang was how much of what she wanted to accomplish was truly her own view of success and how much of it was machinated by those around her in the wake of JAGGED LITTLE PILL's success. One thing I found quite unsettling was the relative timing of the release of Alanis Morissette's album with Ani's own DILATE. Like DILATE, JAGGED LITTLE PILL's best moments come from the observations of a woman in total control of her sexuality and the comfort with which she feels while in control. If Alanis Morissette shocked the world by admitting to having had oral sex in the local Cineplex movie theater, then Ani shocked her coterie of fans by admitting, at least in song, that she was in a heterosexual relationship. If the fractured wails of Alanis's voice made *You Oughta Know* and *Like Rain* anthems of the femme-rocker/punk-poetess/riot-grrl genre, then Ani doing pretty much the same thing on DILATE's superb songs signalled that things weren't ever going to be the same for women who chose heart-on-sleeve lyricism over image for their success. In the wake of JAGGED LITTLE PILL's success, artists who had been making a decent enough living singing heart-on-sleeve music (and I don't mean that in a negative context) soon got lumped in with Alanis Morissette. Before she or Ani knew, they were part of a 'scene', something the media dubbed the "Lilith Fair" movement. It grew and grew, encompassing artists in varied musical settings, people like Sarah McLachlan (of course), Jill Sobule, and Liz Phair. People who remained true to their vision of what they were trying to accomplish. Artists like Ani were judged, unfairly, in the wake of JAGGED LITTLE PILL's success.

The relative success of DILATE (broadening her audience base to a slightly older demographic) and the huge success of JAGGED LITTLE PILL marked turning points for a slew of female artists. In the wake of DiFranco and Morissette came others: Leah Andreone, Jewel Kilcher, Michelle Lewis, Tracy Bonham, Patti Rothberg, Melissa Ferrick, Holly McNarland, and Dayna Manning, to name but a few. All of them are passionate about what it is they want to accomplish. Some are contemporaries of DiFranco, others came after. Yet all of them employ the same basic, folk-angst philosophy which made Ani and Alanis (and Tori Amos) icons of the genre. Towards the end of the book, I've included a discography (purely subjective) of many of these artists. They're central to this story because as Ani's popularity grew, as her profile became mass-media fodder, that same mass-media machine painted an image of women "finally" taking control of their environment. Hogwash and bullshit. We all sell out. But there's a moral value over *how* we sell out. That value becomes a degree. And the women performers who benefitted most from all the attention Ani was getting knew how to make the best of it — just like the so-called 'big boys' did.

That iconography, that sense of being something more than just a recording artist to a generation who, make no mistake, needs heroes (and heroines), accounts for a large part of Ani's success. Like all adored artists, her fan base welcomes her with open arms. Though some might move on with their lives after swallowing all of DiFranco's releases, few are left unfazed by the strong imagery her songs continually conjure up. And for most people aged under twenty, Ani's words are more than merely 'relating', they are the very voice of their own mortal souls as love fractures their hearts, conformity gags and binds their independence, and authority grafts 'the rules' onto their emerging adult lives. In the final analysis, especially for Ani and her understanding fans (as opposed to those who jumped aboard the 'PMS-rock' bandwagon), staying true to the course of being at one with one's self assumed far more importance than the end result of 'net units shipped' and radio-ready airplay. An abject lesson in staying true to your own vision of what you want to accomplish, and of sticking the finger to The Man when He comes a-knockin' to take his cut of your action for himself.

Most of us who aspire to artistic integrity of some form or other frequently 'sell-out' our hopes and dreams in exchange for 'cash' and three weeks at the beach in July. Yet here was someone who did it all by herself when most of us get chewed up by the starmaker machinery. It's important to remember that for anyone in the music industry to thrive is a rarity, let alone be in total control of their art and its conflict/growth with commerce. Because at some point down the assembly line, at some juncture, where the idealism of songwriting becomes the impetus for sales and promotion on a broader scale than culthood, total control shifts hands. And while it's true that many mega-star artists control the making of their music, even the promotion of their image through media means and merchandising, they do not pocket home the full dollar value of their efforts. After the record company skims off its cut, most artists end up making a slightly better than modest income. I underscore the word 'most'. I don't mean the Michael Jacksons and Madonnas of popdom. The Celine Dions and Gloria Estefans. I'm talking about those artists who tour year after year, sell records in modest amounts, who generally have very little (if no) radio support, whose music doesn't regularly get featured on MTV or VH1. By keeping things totally under her own control, Ani pockets home more profit, per item sold, than most major stars. But the ssue. And, in unprecedented fashion, she pumps a fair ofit back into her company while keeping the business falo, New York home town. That's important to Ani. As she retains control over everything she does, she's able to keep the hopes and aspirations of her native home town alive.

How did she do it? How does she *still* do it? She certainly isn't the first female music entrepreneur/record label owner. Isn't the first woman to forge highly personal love/relationship/slice-of-life/agit-prop songs as a means of conveying message and of expressing emotion. Isn't the first person to control it all her own way. But Ani DiFranco steadfastly refuses to give an inch to anyone and has surrounded herself with people she trusts implicitly at record company, distribution, tour, management, and press information levels.

To me, that's a story. But it isn't the only one.

There's the story of Ani DiFranco superstar. The idol of hundreds of thousands of teen-aged girls and Gen-X twentysomethings. In many of her songs Ani despises the trappings of fame and success, yet they are an integral part of becoming successful in the arts. How does she reconcile the two distinct at-odds images her fans make of her. Teens revere her as a Demi-Goddess: a shabby-chic-dressed, nose-ringed Singer Of Songs That Speak Volumes In A Way No One Has Ever Written Before. The fan-as-worshipper-as-stalker mentality. Older fans adore Ani DiFranco in a far more positive manner, appreciating the candor and directness of her music and lyrics. They're Anti-Fans. Praising quietly, religiously, in self-deprecating fashion. They're solitary practitioners and believers. The short hairs on their necks stand on end when they hear yet another Ani-wannabe pontificate about her or genuflect on the Altar of the Demi-Goddess.

Then there's the story of Ani DiFranco the singer-songwriter. The author of witty repartee like *Fuel* and *Names And Dates And Times*. The author of anti-record company diatribes like *The Million You Never Made* and *Napoleon*. The author of *Lost Woman Song*, one of the most poignant songs about pro-choice I've ever heard.

These and much, much more, form the basis of Ani DiFranco. And through it all is the ever-growing sense of being incorporated into something greater than anything she might have envisioned when she set some of her songs to cassette tape in 1990. Through it all is a sense of dread, a fear of guards being let down against the things she despises the most — apathy, abandon, ignorance, complacency.

Listening to Ani DiFranco is like listening to the finest women singer-songwriters of our era. Hers is the voice of Billie Holiday, Odetta, Peggy Seeger, Joan Baez, Joni Mitchell, Sandy Denny, Lucinda Williams, Chrissie Hynde, Edith Piaf, Wendy Waldman, The Roches, Ferron, Joy Of Cooking, Cynthia Mann, Carole King, Patti Smith, Kate Jacobs, Buffy Sainte-Marie, and many, many more. Hearing her words is like taking the pulse of an entire generation born and raised long after the 1960s had burned out: Beth Orton, Amy Rigby, Alanis Morissette, PJ Harvey, Dolores O'Riordan, Susan Werner, Sara Hickman, Liz Phair, Shawn Colvin, Rosanne Cash, Melissa Etheridge, Madonna, Mary Chapin Carpenter, Sinead O'Connor, The McGarrigles, Kate Bush, Courtney Love, Heather Nova, Amanda Marshall, Joan Osborne, Nanci Griffith, Christine Lavin, Bjork, and many others.

Hers is also the voice of Pete Seeger, Woody Guthrie, Neil Young, Bob Dylan, Kurt Cobain, Tom Robinson, Paul Simon, Utah Phillips, Tom Waits, John Lennon, Peter Gabriel, Lou Reed, Loudon Wainwright III, and The Clash's Mick Jones.

It is the sound of being nobody's fool and nobody's baby. Of staying on course through hurricane-level winds. Of fighting the good fight, no matter how fucking tired you are and how futile it all seems.

The sound of righteousness.

Phil Jones presents
an evening with

Ani Difranco

'A TAKE NO SHIT FEMINIST WITH INCREDIBLE MUSICAL ABILITY, RANGING FROM PLAINTIVE FOLK TO ALL OUT ROCK WITH AFRICAN RHYTHMS, HIP HOP, AND SPOKEN WORD THROWN IN'

MUSU Hop & Grape
Tuesday 1st July 1997
7.30pm

Advance tickets £6.50 from
Piccadilly Box Office 0161 832 1111
& SU 0161 275 2930

Souvenirs of Ani's tours and press clippings collected by her fans on the Internet at "Absolute Ani" www.anidifranco.net.

Cover art from Ani's first two albums, featuring her own design on NOT SO SOFT.

Names
And Dates
And Times

ani difranco
c/o righteous babe records
p o box 95, ellicott station, buffalo, ny 14205
phone: (716)852-8020 * fax: (716)852-2741
e-mail: RBRinfo@aol.com

OBJECTIVE
Encouraging resistance and self-empowerment through loud acoustic music.

EDUCATION
Holiday Inn Lounge, Essex Street Pub, Calumet Café, Nietzsche's, & misc. other bars, nightclubs, dumps and dives
  throughout Western New York, ca. 1985-89.
Women's studies coffeehouses and folk festivals, ca. 1989-94.
Colossal temples of rock-n-roll & misc. dumps and dives throughout the world, ca. 1994-present.

Also, skipped classes at:
Buffalo Academy of Visual & Performing Arts, Buffalo, NY, 1984-87 (dance).
Buffalo State College, Buffalo, NY, 1988-89 (painting).
New School For Social Research, NYC, 1990-92 (poetry).

WORK EXPERIENCE
Carpenter, housepainter (Scruffy Dog Painting), waitress, etc., 1985-92.
Singer/songwriter/guitarist, 120+ live shows per year, 1989-present.
CEO, Righteous Babe Records, 14 albums released, 1990-present (dubbed "every major label's worst nightmare"
  by anonymous industry insider).
Producer: ornery albums and rabble-rousing songs by Utah Phillips, Dan Bern, Janis Ian.

EQUIPMENT
Acoustic, tenor, baritone & steel guitars; banjo; mandolin; thumb piano; percussion.

SPECIAL SKILLS
Consistent ability to spread insurrectionist propaganda through mass media (examples: The Late Show with David
  Letterman, Late Night with Conan O'Brien, ABC In Concert, MTV 120 Minutes, VH1 Hard Rock Live).
Targeted surgical strikes via oppositional counter-media (examples: NPR Talk of the Nation, Radio Free Maine,
  Jim Hightower's Chat & Chew Café).
Can tie cherry stem in knot with tongue.

21

DiFranco's life are somewhat shrouded in mystery ation. There is a side to the Ani DiFranco experience that eschews such trite, mundane information as S/A/L (Sex/Age/Location) and pre-artist history. A fair chunk of articles written about Ani and virtually every review of any of her albums almost always fails to mention her origins. When I finally found information about Ani's formative years, it just reinforced my initial impressions.

There's also a fair amount of misinformation. Many of the articles I read gave no real sense of who Ani was, choosing to focus, instead, on the successes of her DIY philosophy. As if she were the only artist in the world to have ever done it that way. A "trailblazer," they often wrote, forgetting that true trailblazers not only operate from without, but also from within. The year Ani was born (1970), there were few out-and-out female rock stars. Opera singers, yes. Pop stars as well. Country stars, for sure. And there were quite a few female folk singers. Most of them survive to this day, continuing to sing about the foibles of man and woman in the face of Company and Satan (sometimes one and the same). But there were very few female rock and rollers. Groups like Fanny and Isis are now long forgotten (despite ex-Fanny member June Millington's post-Fanny success in the Women's Music movement). By the late '70s the landscape had changed thanks to performers like Blondie's Debbie Harry, The Runaways (fronting Joan Jett and Lita Ford), Pat Benatar, Linda Ronstadt, and Suzi Quatro. By the early 1980s, the sight of female-fronted rock groups seemed common enough, yet the entertainment industry still chose to show them as a novelty. The Bangles, The Slits, The Modettes, The Pandoras, the Go-Gos — the New Wave movement had helped break down some of the barriers. But by the middle to the end of the '80s, artists like Tracy Chapman, Michelle Shocked, The Indigo Girls, and Suzanne Vega achieved success and media attention thanks to critical and cult status admiration. The media, ever quick at trying to create something out of nothing, called it The New Folk Revival. A reaction against the so-called "hair-bands" of the start of the decade (think of Bon Jovi, Poison, Twisted Sister).

Ani had the good fortune to meet people like Suzanne Vega and

Michelle Shocked at a time when they were considered critical darlings. She saw the power of the media at a very young age, and that helped foster an image of what she wanted to accomplish and how she was going to do it. By the start of the '90s, at the eager and yet ripe age of 20, the young Ani DiFranco set about going through the traditional route to stardom. She found out the hard way that the industry's mind-set had changed. By 1990, the tide was turning to a heavier form of post-punk pop. Ani, wisely, remained true to her vision and started her own company, choosing to operate just outside accepted norms. By the start of the decade, Ani saw how other female performers worked their way through the industry and found it disheartening. And, as her awareness of her "womanhood" grew (in an artistic sense), she found out that many who had come before her had done it on their own.

Other journalists choose to focus on Ani's 'dyke-hood'. As if it were a badge admitting her to a portion of the market-share not commonly discussed. For a good many years, her world was accepted only by the gay and lesbian communities. The folk community, which had once helped her, shunned her (to a certain degree) when she started grumbling about the inefficiencies of that subculture.

These aspects of Ani DiFranco's story are just as fascinating as the facts about "Mr." DiFranco or the L'il Folksinger, as she sometimes refers to herself. But let's get some of the mundane facts out of the way, the history, then we can let Ani speak about herself, the herstory.

Born on September 23, 1970, Ani DiFranco, the second child of Elizabeth and Dante DiFranco, grew up in a plain, nondescript house in Buffalo, New York. Buffalo had been built on the backs and hands and sweat and toil of steel workers, of manufacturing companies whose profits took a slide downwards in the 1970s. Plant closures and relocations took their toll on this proud town they call The Queen City. And, all jokes aside about the fires the city is rather infamous for, Buffalo boasts a sizable music following. Groups like Mercury Rev, Goo Goo Dolls, and others have kept the entertainment fires burning throughout the 1970s, '80s, '90s.

Dad was a research engineer with a degree from MIT (Massachusetts Institute of Technology). Her mother, who had been raised in my home town, Montreal, was also studying at MIT (in the architecture faculty, one of the few women to do so at the time) when she met Dante. Dante, Ani will tell you, is a calm man. Elizabeth, a motorcycle-riding firebrand unafraid of telling people exactly how she felt. "My dad . . . he doesn't impose himself on anybody. He's very quiet and stoic," Ani stated during an interview in *Diva*. Her mother, Ani explains, is different: "She's very flaming. She now lives with me in my house and I find it hard to talk to her. I left home young and made her into a hero. I always thought of her as being very independent, funny and strong. Now I know more about her and there's a lot that scares me, that it might be in myself, because she's totally nuts."

Both mom and dad were professional people and were rarely home after school. So, at a very young age, Ani learned to fend for herself — a 'latchkey' child. These days, leaving an eight-year-old at home to fend for herself after school seems to smack of abandonment, but in the late 1970s, it was still a rather everyday thing to do for kids whose parents were both unavailable come the end of the school day. I know, I was one myself. This sense of independence is both comforting to a young soul and unsettling. It's that sense of being old enough to do things on your own, but being young enough to resent having to do them at all. Instead, it gave the youngster much needed gumption on running the world in her own way. As Ani comments in the Marc Woodworth edited book *Solo: Women Singer-Songwriters in Their Own Words*, "I'm used to being independent and calling all the shots, so none of this is odd to me. I was pretty much on my own from the time I was a kid because in my family I was the one who wasn't in trouble. I was well adjusted, so I was easily overlooked. My mother and father afforded me a lot of independence and just assumed I would rise to the occasion. It was a really good way for me to be brought up — or not brought up, as the case may be — because I was always a very independent person, the stable one in a very fucked-up family . . . I was pretty fearless. I always had big balls. My parents instilled that kind of independence in me. And I was a happy kid even though I'm sure I shouldn't have been. That independence allowed me to deal with the fact that everything's always in flux."

Her parents had no doubt they were dealing with a smart, precocious child who knew how to handle herself. They left her alone most of the time. When Ani started including music in her lifestyle, her parents didn't rebel or have shit-fits, especially her mother. "I think she always treated me with respect," Ani told Ms., "even though she was a parent. Actually, when I was younger, she was the heavy. My father was laissez-faire about parenting. . . . My mother was very strict when I was growing up and then at some point she was like 'Well, you're a person and I respect you.' She always fed me this 'You can do whatever you want' kind of thing and I bought it. It's crazy shit to tell a kid, but she was always incredibly supportive, one of those parents who thought whatever I did was fabulous. Right from the beginning she was the one person who always said, I trust your judgment." They chose to give her room to roam and steered clear. Ani believes that it was this sense of independence which made her what she is. She felt that there was no judgment, no stifling, no roadblocks.

Ani remembers the early years being filled with the usual family politics. "The house, when everyone lived together, was like one scary scene after another," she said in her 1996 Ms. interview. "So it was a good thing we all kind of went our separate ways." But there was more.

At age nine she got a Beatles guitar and started learning songs (like Ob-La-Di, Ob-La-Da) without any professional or formal education (she did start taking lessons later). Again, she had to figure it out on her own. "I remember telling my parents I wanted to play guitar. I don't know where I got that idea from because it wasn't like the old musical family situation," Ani's been quoted as saying. "And I didn't really have that rock and roll dream either. I certainly didn't have that. It wasn't like I wanted to be a rock star. I just wanted a guitar." When she finally decided to take lessons, she went to a local music shop and walked in without appointment. It was at this shop that she met Michael Meldrum, a local musician, music teacher, and promoter who noticed Ani waiting for a guitar lesson. He saw a sweet girl with a wondrous smile and asked her to play a song for him. Jethro Tull's Wond'ring Aloud and W.C. Handy's St. Louis Blues were the songs Ani chose to play. "She had a great voice, a big voice coming out of this very little person," Meldrum told Ellen Papazian in the November 1996 Ms. "And she was really working hard at playing the difficult parts of these songs. She wasn't a hack. She was always interested in how the guitar worked."

A year later, Ani and Meldrum had become friends with Meldrum booking her into venues wherever and whenever he could. People were often shocked at seeing the two of them together, the mentor in his thirties with a mere "babe in the woods" by his side, carrying a guitar almost as big as she was. It caused quite a stir as Meldrum booked her in local bars and watering spots. "I'd show up with my 'guardian' Mike. . . . He was an alcoholic barfly folk singer who was my best friend. I was always precocious, so when I was on my own at 15, I made an agreement with bar owners that I'd get to play but wouldn't drink," Ani once told a reporter for *The San Francisco Chronicle.*

As Ani learned to play guitar, her involvement with Meldrum led to the DiFranco household becoming a sort of "drop-in" center for folk singers who were touring and needed a stop in the Buffalo area. Imagine the influence on your life having a parade of modern folk singers walking in and out of your living room, people like John Gorka, Rod Anderson, Christine Lavin, Cheryl Wheeler, Suzanne Vega, Michelle Shocked. People at the start of their careers and industry veterans. "Quite a few of them stayed at my family's house because he (Meldrum) always needed some place to put them," Ani told *Dirty Linen.* "I got to know them way back when and I was hanging out with a bunch of singer-songwriters." Suzanne Vega recalls striking up a friendship with the precocious ten-year-old and worried that Ani was hanging around with a fast crowd. "Ani had this hyperanimation which she still has now," Vega told *Ms.* "I used to see her at a club where we would all play, even after I stopped staying at her house. I remember being concerned for her because she was running with a fast crowd."

"I had to get out of the house so I went and hung out in these circles, and I started playing guitar," Ani told *Ms.* "I learned you could write songs for a living, which is not something they teach you in school."

By the time she'd reached eleven, Ani DiFranco was already a seasoned stage veteran, performing before small crowds in intimate university settings, entertaining larger crowds at folk festivals, and paying her dues at local dives before the normal group of unruly patrons. Ani credits her sharp, angular, percussive guitar style with playing in loud bars where you had to be a little bit louder than the patrons in order to be heard. And she made sure she was heard. As Ani told *The San Francisco Chronicle,* "I've seen *MTV Unplugged,* a bunch of guys sitting on stools acting as if they discovered something new by playing acoustic. But what's so big about going electric and turning your amp all the way up? I can get a lot more energy and power and emotion by not plugging in. I wanted claws to hit the strings harder, so I use plastic fingernails that I tape to my fingers to keep from bloodying myself." This rough and tumble way of performing would prove invaluable at the start of her 'professional' career. Of her playing, she told *Guitar Player*, "It was a survival technique. It evolved out of twelve years of playing in bars, where people are there to pick up somebody and drink themselves into a stupor, not to listen to the chick in the corner with the acoustic."

Eventually, she met others her own age and began performing in a band, though she claims to have forgotten the name of the band, brushing those years off the way few artists do when they reminisce about their first group experience. "When I was sixteen, I played in a band," Ani stated in an interview for *Monkey Magnet* in November 1995. "We didn't really have a name. We were kind of a house band at the Essex Street Pub. It's a place that holds like 20 people and it's in a nowhere neighborhood in Buffalo. I was the songwriter . . . I was like 'suck girl'."

But her true calling (as she stated in her *Ms.* interview) was dance. She soon lost interest in the guitar and spent the next few years honing her dancing skills. Her bio, made up to look like a resume, proudly states under the "Education" heading, "skipped classes at The Buffalo Academy of Visual & Performing Arts." She stayed there until 1987. However, when Ani was fourteen and while on summer vacation, she picked up her guitar and started noodling around. Problem was, she couldn't remember any of the songs she'd learned earlier. And, being a teenager with a disintegrating home life, it didn't take her long to find inspiration in her day-to-day world. The muse had taken over and Ani started writing and performing her own songs. "For me to start writing songs seemed like the thing to do at the time because everybody else was doing it," she told *Dirty Linen*. She played them to Meldrum who wasted no time booking her for more concerts and events. She performed in a variety of settings, from Holiday Inns to the Essex Street Pub, from coffee houses like The Calumet Café to night clubs like Nietzsche's. Her resume states she also performed in "other bars, nightclubs, dumps and dives throughout Western New York" from 1985 to 1989.

At fifteen, Ani's parents divorced: Elizabeth moved to Connecticut,

Dante remained in Buffalo. Ani, not wanting to create any further chasms between herself and her parents, chose to strike out on her own. "I didn't see it as a big tragic story or a big leap," Ani stated during her *Sessions At West 54th* interview. "It was just kind of like, well, do you want to live with your dad, or you want to go move in the woods with your mom? So I just get a little apartment and make do." She took up a variety of jobs to give her cash while still completing school. "I had an afternoon job after high school. I was a candy striper. . . . I have had the most veritable cornucopia of service industry jobs." Waitressing, house painting, on-site construction work. It was there that she met future manager Scot Fisher. Fisher, then a carpenter, hired Ani to haul plaster buckets from house renovation projects. At that time, he was also studying law.

While balancing school and work, Ani performed Saturday nights at local bars. In 1986 she graduated from high school. Her teen years were plagued with a souring relationship with a man (far older than her). She became pregnant and her 'friend' abandoned her altogether after her abortion. Ani documents her feelings and reactions unflinchingly on her own *Lost Woman Song* from the first album.

> i opened a bank account
> when i was nine years old
> i closed it when i was eighteen
> i gave them every penny that i'd saved
> and they gave my blood and urine a number
> now i'm sitting in the waiting room
> playing with the toys
> i am here to exercise my freedom of choice
> i passed their hand held signs
> i went through their picket lines
> they gathered when they saw me coming
> they shouted when they saw me cross
> i said why don't you go home
> just leave me alone
> i'm just another woman lost . . .

his bored eyes were obscene
on his denimed thighs a magazine
i wish he'd never come here with me
in fact i wish he'd never come near me
i wish his shoulder wasn't touching mine
i am growing older waiting in this line
but some of life's best lessons
are learned at the worst of times
under the fierce fluorescent
she offered her hand for me to hold
she offered stability and calm
and i was crushing her palm
through the pinch pull wincing
my smile unconvincing
on that sterile battlefield that sees
only casualties
never heroes
my heart hit absolute zero
lucille, your voice still sounds in me
mine was a relatively easy tragedy
the profile of our country
looks a little less hard-nosed
but that picket line persisted
and that clinic has since been closed
they keep pounding their fists on reality
hoping it will break
but i don't think that there's one of them
who leads a life free of mistakes

(from *Lost Woman Song*, 1990)

During this time Ani also attended Buffalo State College from 1988 to 1989 and studied painting and art while continuing to write and perform her songs wherever she could. "There's not a lot of action in Buffalo," Ani said during her *Sessions at West 54th* interview, "but it's a very unpretentious town, you know, people are friendly. I think a lot of the way I do things is, you know, the Buffalo in me. It's just this hard knock town that the steel plant moved out of a long time ago. So, the glamor of musicianship in Buffalo is playing in little dive bars. I ran an open mike for years, you know, and played every Saturday night at the Essex Street Pub and you make your twenty bucks and then you go back to your real job. That's the way it is." By the time she had turned seventeen, she had determined that she would strike out on her own and try to get signed to a recording label. "I considered sending it out when I was 17 or 18. I made my first album, and my manager thought he'd shop it around the labels," Ani told *The Advocate*'s Achy Obejas. "Meanwhile, I just kept making albums. My indie philosophy developed over the years as I focused on my politics. I talked to this one indie label — they were small, they seemed like 'OK, let's go out, drink some beer, talk politics.' I thought, this could be cool. Then I got the contract and I said, 'This is not cool. This is fucked.' It made me realize the music business is a business like any other and the focus is profit." The majors either turned her down or ignored her, having already signed acts like The Indigo Girls and Tracy Chapman. It was the late 1980s, the tail-end of the big hair bands, the start of grunge. The public had seemingly had it with sensitive female singer-songwriters.

This Do It Yourself (DIY) ethic wasn't particularly new. Fugazi, a well respected punk band, had kept total control of their records, promotion, marketing, et cetera while forming their own label (Dischord) and allowing no major any piece of their action. Crass, another band from England, had done the same thing for the entirety of their recording careers. It's not doubtful that a young Ani, disillusioned with a business that was all hype and golden handshakes, would have known about Fugazi and their DIY ethos. Whether she did or didn't, Ani chose, in the end, to strike out on her own and start up her own record company.

In 1989 she met Dale Anderson, a 47-year-old rock critic based in New York who had learned of her impending move to the Big Apple. Anderson felt she was better than virtually anyone else he was hearing at the time and took an active interest in her career. He made sure she got in touch with a lawyer and learned the ins and outs of negotiating, to make sure Ani was totally in touch with all her options and controlling her own destiny. "I was afraid someone was going to come and rip her to shreds," he stated in Papazian's *Ms.* interview.

Ani moved to New York City in 1989, to attend the New School for Social Research (she stayed until 1992, specializing in poetry) and to expose her songwriting and performing skills to a broader range of people. One of her New School instructors, poet Sekou Sundiata, soon became her mentor. Years later, she would pay homage to the instructor's tutelage by signing Sundiata to a recording contract with Righteous Babe Records. Quietly, surely, determinedly, Ani was getting her songs heard in her own way, despite very little radio airplay or mass media attention.

By decade's end, Ani felt the time was right to release her own recordings on her own label. In the *Hero Magazine* article by Jeffrey L. Newman titled "Queer Girls from Buffalo," Ani recalled, "It seemed like even the good guys were handing out bad contracts. I just decided I didn't need it that bad. It turns out I was right, but I got lucky. I decided it wasn't worth it to me to compromise myself personally or artistically. I didn't want to work with business people in my life. The people who run record companies are not the hippest or grooviest people. They might have pony-tails, but they're business people. Their opinions are opposite mine. I started questioning immediately, 'Why can't I do this myself?'" Trying to go the major label route seemed both futile and unsatisfactory. The aim was to press up cassettes of songs she had been working on and performing for a while. By 1989, she had written over 100 songs, each framed in personal lyricism and a strong sense of melody based on folk, punk, and rock. Some claimed her guitar stylings were patterned after those of Michael Hedges, a respected performer whose recordings with Windham Hill helped create so-called New Age music. And while Ani may have heard of Hedges or even heard his guitar work, she denies he had a major impact on the way she plays.

In September of 1990, Ani DiFranco entered Audio Magic Studio in Buffalo, recorded a dozen of the hundred plus songs she'd written over the previous five years, and borrowed the $1500.00 needed to record, duplicate, and prepare 500 cassettes (some accounts list the number as 300) for release. She decided to call her fledgling company Righteous Babe Records. "Righteous" because it's what she felt and "Babe" based on what her and a girlfriend buddy of hers used to call each other. (At first she had intended on calling her company just "Righteous Records" but changed her mind when she learned a Southern U.S. gospel label had rights to the name.) And, before the album was finished, she had walked to Buffalo City Hall to lay down $50.00 to register the label's name. Ani, Dale, and Scot settled on a Buffalo company, Eastern Standard Productions, to handle the task of pressing and duplicating Ani's releases. Mark Mekker and wife Deborah, acquaintances of Scot Fisher's, were only too happy to get the business (and remain, to this day, affiliated with RBR by continuing to manufacture the label's cassettes and CDs). Ani set about selling the tapes at her shows. Quickly she sold out of the first batch and found the need to produce more. Righteous Babe, the company, was operated from Buffalo, but Ani still ran it from her New York apartment. "It was a joke in the beginning," Ani told Ms., "very theoretical, like 'I have my own record company,' which means that I just put out a tape independently."

In September, ANI DIFRANCO (RBR-001) was released. It contained twelve songs, all performed by Ani solo on guitar. The album was produced by Ani and Dale Anderson (who had "managed" Ani's career following her split with Michael Meldrum). John Caruso engineered the session. Ani wrote four sentences for the release which appeared on the cassette (and later the CD) graphic: "I speak without reservation from what I know and who I am. I do so with the understanding that all people should have the right to offer their voice to the chorus whether the result is harmony or dissonance, the worldsong is a colorless dirge without the differences which distinguish us, and it is that difference which should be celebrated not condemned. Should any part of my music offend you, please do not close your ears to it. Just take what you can use and go on."

From the first note of *Both Hands* to the closing second of *Out Of Habit*, her debut attracted the attention of local press and a young college and university-oriented crowd who had known of her music through her coffee-house tours. Songs like *Both Hands*, about the intimate moments of lovemaking (between two women), first endeared her to the lesbian community.

. . . both hands
now use both hands
no don't close your eyes
i am writing
graffiti on your body
i am drawing the story
of how hard we tried
i am watching your chest rise and fall
like the tides of my life
and the rest of it all
your bones have been my bed frame
and your flesh has been my pillow
i've been waiting for sleep
to offer up the deep with both hands
in each other's shadow we grew less and less tall
and eventually our theories couldn't explain it all
so I'm recording our history
now on the bedroom wall
and when we leave the landlord will come
and paint over it all

(from *Both Hands*, 1990)

"A fine debut from this young songwriter, singer and guitarist," a reviewer in *Ladyslipper* wrote (reprinted here from *All Music Guide*), "whose songs and poems are literate, melodic, feminist, well-arranged and full of meaningful imagery. Plus, she's got a lovely, versatile voice." Ira Robbins, editor of the *Trouser Press Guide To 90's Rock*, was also quick to praise Ani. "A skilled guitar plucker with an athletic voice, an infectious laugh, appealing melodies and the lyrical acuity to (usually) resist the sophomoric preciousness that afflicts other sensitive young singer/songwriters. DiFranco ambles easily on the creative waters that have drowned so many in crocodile tears."

But the album wasn't strictly created with the lesbian community in mind. Slowly, steadily, cassette tape dubs of her recordings were made and passed around by adoring fans who wanted to share the Ani experience with friends, families, and loved ones. Daughters made dubs for their mothers, sisters for their older/younger siblings, lovers to lovers, friends to friends. Ani started to get out-of-town mail asking her to perform in various cities and venues, at places where appreciative audiences would come and hear her heart-on-sleeve, this-is-my-life lyrics, finding in her music the voice of a sister, a lover, a friend. That communal sense of sharing continues to this day as tape traders exchange bootlegs of Ani concerts they've attended with other fans who've made their own tapes.

The cassette continued to sell, allowing Ani to reprint it repeatedly. By 1990 and the start of a new decade, Ani was well on her way to becoming the L'il Folksinger.

"I'VE GOT HIGHWAYS FOR STRETCHMARKS"

Ani's emerging years, the ones where she was followed and adored by a small coterie of fans, saw her expand her touring base from the Buffalo area to New England, the Mid-Atlantic states, and, eventually, Texas and California. For many years, she toured virtually on her own, just her and her guitar, criss-crossing the continent in her car to any gig that paid decently.

Ani once described a typical performance (this time in Texas) during her interview in Ms. as performing to "six or seven cowboys and one chick. . . . I stood in the corner and played for an hour. When I finished, the woman started screaming and yelling and hooting. I remember the triumphant feeling I had when I left the bar, clutching my 20 bucks and knowing I'd won over a fan. I thought, 'Wow, somebody really heard something there. There is some value to what I'm doing.' It seemed like a small victory."

Ani received many letters from fans who had heard her tape (often as a duplicate of a duplicate of an original tape purchased by someone at one of her shows) and had found enough people interested in seeing her as to warrant Ani traveling 'there'. From the sale of her recordings, she earned enough money to buy a Volkswagen Beetle, and used it constantly to get from gig to gig. Shows were held in concert halls, college dorms, clubs, bars, parlor-halls. Wherever women wanted her to play, Ani went. Dale Anderson became her personal manager and oversaw gigs and bookings while they operated Righteous Babe out of her New York apartment on Avenue D in the city's Lower East Side, where she continued to go to school and also worked for a Central American Solidarity movement and the War Resisters' League between the gigs which soon filled her calendar.

"Letters would start to come in from colleges," Ani told *Dirty Linen*. "So I started to travel, because students would organize to get me to play at their school in New Jersey or upstate New York or Pennsylvania and that's how touring started. I was leaving town on the weekends to play shows, the weekends started getting longer and longer, and pretty soon I dropped out of school." She got to see much of America in a direct manner, driving behind the wheel of her car in total abandon to the elements, the state of roads and her vehicle, cops who didn't quite know what to make of her waifish yet decidedly big-city attitude and presence, and people in small towns unaccustomed to same. "The life of a folksinger," Ani told *Option Magazine* in 1994, "you stay in a lot of people's houses, pet a lot of people's cats, and you're gone the next day. You get to look at a lot of vignettes of people's lives, snippets of what their lives are like. You sort of enter into their realm for a few hours and then you're gone. It's sort of like the world as a movie and never quite being a part of it," a sentiment that informs the lyrics of *Every State Line*, her peculiar take on the standard rock 'n' roll road song.

i got pulled over in west texas
so they could look inside my car
he said are you an american citizen
i said, yes sir, so far
they made sure i wasn't smuggling
someone in from mexico
someone willing to settle for america
because there's nowhere else to go
every state line
there's a new set of laws
and every police man

comes equipped with extended claws
there's a thousand shades of white
and a thousand shades of black
but the same rule always applies
smile pretty and watch your back

i broke down in louisiana
and i had to thumb a ride
got in the first car that pulled over
you can't be picky in the middle of the night
he said baby do you like to fool around
baby do you like to be touched
i said maybe some other time
fuck you very much . . .

(from *Every State Line*, 1992)

For 200 out of 365 days, Ani toured the continent in her 1969 VW bug with just her guitar and her l'il ole self. "I can't think of another way of doing it that would still have life in it," she told *Option Magazine*. "I've got highways for stretch marks."

Folk festivals, coffee-house performances, college stages, nightclubs and bars were her terrain; her guitar, her voice, her presence were her tools of conquest. As her name and reputation grew, her appearances at a large number of folk festivals were pivotal to her success and her emerging career. In 1991, Ani appeared at the Mariposa Folk Festival at Ontario Place in Toronto. 1992 saw her appear at the Vancouver, Calgary, Philadelphia, and Blue Skies Folk Festivals. She performed in 1993 at the Appel Farm Folk Festival (Elmer, New Jersey), the Winnipeg Folk Festival, the Edmonton Folk Festival, and the Michigan Womyn's Folk, where, as Ani commented to Achy Obejas of *The Advocate*, "They didn't know what to make of me. . . . I felt like there was a certain language barrier. Everyone was razzing my friend. She was wearing a T-shirt with The Texas Tornadoes (the legendary Tex-Mex country-rock band led by the late Doug Sahm). People said stuff like, 'Turn it around or take it off — it has pictures of men.'" Being a "womyn" seemed at odds with her street-tough humor. Ani also participated in a number of Mountain Stage Festival appearances, some of which were recorded and made available on recordings issued by Oh Boy Records.

Her second album, NOT SO SOFT, released in 1991, was well received by music critic Ira Robbins. "DiFranco's second album . . . is true to its title. Besides adding some conga drum and overdubs she replaces the pretty folksinging of the debut with a forceful, vibrato-curdled blues-rock voice and attacks her guitar with the percussive vigor of someone who has played too many noisy crowds without an amplifier." In his final assessment, "too many songs overreach and bellyflop in mostly mushy ground." The album, however, saw Ani again revealing herself sexually, in a lesbian context, on songs like *Itch*, *She Says*, and *Make Me Stay*, even bisexually, in the song *The Whole Night*.

> we can touch
> touch our girl cheeks
> and we can hold hands
> like paper dolls
> we can try
> try each other on
> in the privacy
> within new york city's walls
> we can kiss
> kiss goodnight
> and we can go home wondering
> what would it be like if
> if I did not have a boyfriend
> and we could spend
> the whole night . . .

(from *The Whole Night*, 1991)

As her 'womyn' fans got to know her better through these songs, they only became more earnest in their appreciation, elevating her to a superhero realm, much to the surprise of the L'il Folksinger.

IN OR OUT

During the early '90s, Ani kept a steady (if somewhat frantic) pace of touring and releasing albums. IMPERFECTLY was released in 1992, featuring such songs as *I'm No Heroine*, perhaps a reply to her fans who were beginning to invest too much of themselves in her, but also a candid statement of her purpose in writing songs.

you think i wouldn't have him
unless i could have him by the balls
you think i just dish it out
you don't think i take it at all
you think i am stronger
you think i walk taller than the rest
you think i'm usually wearing the pants
just cause i rarely wear a dress
well . . .

when you look at me
you see my purpose you see my pride
you think i just saddle up my anger
and ride and ride
you think i stand so firm
you think i sit so high on my trusty steed
let me tell you
i'm usually face down on the ground
when there's a stampede

i'm no heroine
least not last time i checked
i'm too easy to roll over
i'm too easy to wreck
i just write about what
i should have done

i sing what i wish i could say
and i hope somewhere
some woman hears my music
and it helps her through the day . . .

(from *I'm No Heroine*, 1992)

IMPERFECTLY was well received critically. *Ladyslipper*'s AMG review reads: "With her third album, Ani achieves a level of intensity that folk-rock rarely reaches. Unflinching in her pursuit of honesty, she strikes sparks incessantly as she challenges sexual politics, social conventions, and the meaning of existence. Including her own. . . . For the first time, other musicians appear as accompanists, adding shadings of viola, trumpet, mandolin."

By 1993 Ani's on-my-own stance started to get to her, as she explained in *Chart*. "I was my own roadie, guitar tech, road manager and driver. You can only do that for so many years at the kind of pace that I was doing it at, and then you start to go nuts. I was given point-blank financial advice from my manager: 'If you make and sell T-shirts, you can afford to have help on the road.' So we had to do it. But not my name; I wasn't going to put my name or face on them. Those are my rules. So I thought I'd just print some poetry on them."

In 1993, Ani hired people to work for Righteous Babe and decided to relocate the company to Buffalo. Dale Anderson left Righteous Babe Records and quit being Ani's manager in 1994. By then, Scot Fisher had already stepped into the role of being Ani's best friend, her personal manager, and — eventually — the president of Righteous Babe Records (Ani is CEO). Fisher, whose law experiences had led him into working with prisoners in Texas, is devoted to Ani. Both share the same vision, and while Fisher may feel she should play the rock 'n' roll 'game' a little more readily than Ani feels she should, he respects her opinions and doesn't push her into doing things she feels uncomfortable doing. To this day, Ani calls the shots with regards to all media interviews. She'll do only the ones she feels have merit, declining invitations from self-serving radio stations.

"As I started touring more and selling more records . . . more stores started picking them up, you know, and little regional distributors started to distribute my records," Ani said during her *Sessions At West 54th* interview. "So I got more and more help friend by friend, and now we have an office and a coffee machine and a key to the bathroom, you know. But we didn't start out with stationery or anything. It was just me."

With the release of PUDDLE DIVE, her fourth album in three years, Ani's popularity grew. In an interview in *Ms.*, she traced her career to this stage. "The audience over the years broadened and I moved out of that circuit into this general folk music circuit and festivals. Then I moved from there into the rock 'n' roll world, but now all these women who have been around since the beginning – young women who invested a lot emotionally in my work – feel that they have a claim on me. And everything I do now is suspect. For as many people who say, wow, that's great, there are many critics." One of the most insightful and entertaining songs on the album is *Names And Dates And Places*, which Ani wrote in response to her performances on the folk-festival circuit. "It's amazing," she told *Option Magazine*, "you go to a folk festival and there's so many white people out in the field that it's hard to keep track of them all. I mean, I like folk music because it tends to span generations, but it does tend to be a white thing and that's kind of a drag. It's a drag that the world is so segregated. . . . I'm never quite sure if I'm a freak at the folk festival or some chick with an acoustic guitar at a rock club."

> i know so many white people
> i mean where do i start
> the trouble with white people
> is you just can't tell them apart
> i'm so bad with names
> and dates and times
> but i'm big on faces
> that is except for mine . . .
>
> i am so many white people
> i mean where do i start
> i got lots of personalities
> i just can't tell them apart

and i never remember anything
except for those things that I never forget
there's no in between
i'm big on your face
yeah it's big in my mind
you're like the rest of the human race
you are one of a kind.

(from *Names And Dates And Places*, 1993)

PUDDLE DIVE was greeted with critical praise by Ira Robbins: "What were tentative band experiments on IMPERFECTLY become the rule on PUDDLE DIVE. . . . The rich, playful album is marbled with tasteful instrumental contributions that fill in the tracks but stay out of the star's way."

With the success of her fourth album came the attentions of major record companies at last. One of the first to pay attention to Ani was Mercury Records. Danny Goldberg, then the CEO of Mercury, stated in *Ms.*, "She's one of the most brilliant and compelling artists out now . . . a genius." Mercury tried to sign Ani, but nothing much came of it, for reasons Ani alludes to in her *West 54th* interview: "For me it was always a political thing, you know. I just don't like big money capitalism. I don't like big corporations. I think that record companies are there to make money. They could be selling microchips or oil, or whatever. It's just CDs you know. And I'm not interested in partnering up, as you say, with people who have that kind of mentality. It's just big business. And I'm much more interested in art and social movements, and music that's created outside of that corporate structure. I kind of grew up in the folk music world, and there's so much beautiful music that's made without a commercial thought, you know, and that's the way I want to live. And I just felt like there's no way that you can live that way and work on a major label." The corporate executives at the major record companies might have seen this response to their overtures coming if they had listened to such songs as *Napoleon* on her DILATE album and especially *Blood in the Boardroom* on PUDDLE DIVE. Ani is not a fan of corporate America, to say the least.

sitting in the boardroom
the i'm so bored room
listening to the suits talk about their world
they can make straight lines out of almost anything
except for the line of my upper lip when it curls . . .
i wonder can these boys smell me bleeding thru my underwear
there's men wearing the blood of the women they love
there's white wearing the blood of the brown
but every women learns how to bleed from the moon
and we bleed to renew life every time it's cut down . . .
i say it ain't no hassle, it ain't no mess
right now it's the only power that i possess
these business men got the money
they got the instruments of death
but i can make life i can make breath
sitting in the boardroom
the i'm so bored room
i didn't really have much to say the whole time i was there
so i just left a big brown stain on their white chair

(from *Blood In The Boardroom*, 1993

An invitation from California concert promoter Tracye Lawson led to a tour of the Southwest, and her growing on-stage concerts (now occasionally including the rudimentaries of a band) allowed the musician that was Ani room to mature and grow. In June of 1993, Ani entered Select Sound Studio in Keamore, New York and re-recorded fifteen tracks which had been previously released on her first two albums. Scot Fisher contributed some piano and accordion and other musicians assisted throughout. But the main focus was on Ani's growth as a performer. Her years of travel had given the songs added depth and she wanted to give them a different lustre. "On the first two albums," Ani told *Dirty Linen*, "I never really did play with the songs in terms of other instrumentation. Listening back on the first album and the second album, a little bit less, I think I hadn't found my own voice yet. To me I sound not quite like me and so I wanted to re-record certain songs on the first two albums that are still alive for me and bring them up-to-date in terms of how I play them now as opposed to four years ago." LIKE I SAID (SONGS 1990-1991) received fine reviews and allowed fans the chance to catch up with Ani's earlier pieces, notably, again, from Ira Robbins: "DiFranco's growth as a thoughtful, expressive singer informs the delicate, intimate reconsiderations. The effect is subtle but marvelous."

During one of her early '90s shows, Ani met another man who would prove to be important in her growth as a musician. Canadian drummer Andy Stochansky had achieved a reputation as a solid drummer and had worked with noted spoken-word/multi-media artist Meryn Cadell, North York nice-boys The Barenaked Ladies, cult-hero Jonathan Richman, and DiFranco's buddies Amy Ray and Emily Saliers of The Indigo Girls. Ani opened a Buffalo concert for cellist Anne Bourne featuring Andy on drums. Three months after the gig, Andy got a call from RBR and was asked to play on PUDDLE DIVE. "In 90, 91 there really weren't that many angry chick singers with guitars doing things in an independent way," Stochansky told Now's Kim Hughes in September 1999 (on the occasion of the launch of his second solo album). "I wanted it to work just to stick it to all those groups that have millions of dollars and suck so hard. So I just thought, 'What a perfect band for me to be in.' And it was intense, because you knew these women coming to the shows really wanted a voice." The experience benefitted both artists. Ani got to add a deeper, more tribal sound to her repertoire; Stochansky was able to hone his talents and performed with Ani for eight years. While Stochansky no longer tours with Ani, his split from what he termed "the Ani army" was amicable.

Ani's album OUT OF RANGE was released in 1994. Tour dates continued unabated and a booking agency, Fleming/Tamulevich, was retained to organize Ani's shows. Critics were ever more praiseworthy. CMJ reviewer Megan McLaughlin wrote: "Like Liz Phair's songs, Ani DiFranco's music punches folk/angst buttons, confronting personal sexual issues in a quiet atmosphere. On OUT OF RANGE, DiFranco fleshes out her spare vocal/acoustic guitar dynamic with the sporadic addition of drums, piano, bass and accordion. It's on the quieter songs, however, that DiFranco's rough approach and sweet melodies blend into their finest vintage. Throughout, DiFranco's sharp way, both with her lyrics and her self-examination, is the guiding point. . . . Although it's too presumptuous to declare female folk artists such as Liz Phair the beacon of a wider trend, Ani DiFranco's OUT OF RANGE is a welcome addition to that select crowd." For Ira Robbins, "OUT OF RANGE is DiFranco's masterpiece, a fully primed band (and solo) effort that delivers her into the real world with an established and presentably commercial sound, a clear artistic vision and a secure sense of place."

If her lyrics on songs like *The Diner* or *Buildings And Bridges* seemed too slice-of-life for some, it didn't phase Ani one bit. "Everybody assumes that there are some secrets you only tell very few people," Ani told *Monkey Magnet* in 1995, "there's lots of our experience that is taboo and that can't be shared because it's inappropriate in mixed company and years ago I gave that all up. It's like, fuck that! That is just cowardice to me and it's useless. I mean, to me there's no such thing as private or personal. It's all universal. It's all eternal and we share so many experiences that we just don't admit to and we don't about them. I used to think 'Oh my God, I can't sing this, look, my father's here.' Or I'd feel, you know, really funny about talking about certain experiences I've had. But I mean, that was a long time ago and now I'm like 'Oh get over it!'" She also nailed down perfectly her image as spokesperson for her generation of women in *Face Up And Sing*.

> some guy tried to rub up against me
> on a crowded subway car
> some guy tried to feed me some stupid line
> in some stupid bar
> i see the shit every day
> the landscape looks so bleak
> i think i'll take the first one home
> that does something unique
>
> some chick says
> thank you for saying all the things I never do
> i say you know the thanks i get

is to take all the shit for you
it's nice that you listen
it'd be nicer if you joined in
as long as you play their game girl
you're never going to win . . .

(from *Face Up And Sing*, 1994)

Ani's first overseas concert came in late 1994 when she traveled to England, appearing at Upstairs At The Garage in London. She returned to England in March 1995 as the opening act for noted Celtic-rockers Oysterband and Mean Fiddler. 1995 also saw Ani travel to Australia for an appearance at the Woodford Folk Festival.

In 1995/96 she released two albums, both of which would prove to be breakthrough releases: NOT A PRETTY GIRL and DILATE. Both albums deal with important issues in Ani's life: her sexuality and the way others paint her and how she wants to *not* be pigeonholed by any one community. "Unplugged and uncompromising, the 24 year old singer/songwriter is a steadfast independent," wrote *CMJ*'s Jenny Eliscu in a 1995 review of NOT A PRETTY GIRL. "The non-conformity that characterizes her songwriting style spilling over into her career decisions . . . she remains as dynamic and original as ever. The common thread in all her songs remains her point-blank lyrics; her confessional style affords us an unusual (if at times uncomfortable) closeness to the artist."

Both albums were tied up in "is-she-isn't-she" rhetoric as Ani continued to be "ambivalent" about her sexuality. "I guess (I'm) bisexual," Ani told *The Advocate*. "I'm so used to that label, but I always call myself queer. I like the word *queer*, 'cause it sounds funny, queer ha-ha. It's a cool word. It means, like, the kind of love I experience is not the kind of love that's on TV. It's funny. Often love — the politicization of love — is so claustrophobic for people on any side of the equation. In the dyke community, your love affair is a political statement; you can't avoid the politics. But sometimes it's like everyone forgets the real purpose of being with this person." This opinion found its way dramatically into her song *In Or Out* from IMPERFECTLY a few years earlier, with her play between a "miss difranco" and "mr. difranco" personae.

guess there's something wrong with me
guess i don't fit in
no one wants to touch it
no one knows where to begin
i've got more than one membership
to more than one club
and i owe my life
to the people that i love

he looks me up and down
like he knows what time it is
like he's got my number
like he thinks it's his
he says call me miss difranco
if there's anything I can do
i say it's mr. difranco to you

some days the line i walk
turns out to be straight
other days the line tends to deviate
i've got no criteria for sex or race
i just want to hear your voice
i just want to see your face

she looks me up and down
like she thinks that i'll mature
like she's got my number
like it belongs to her
she says call me ms. difranco
if there's anything i can do
i say i've got spots
i've got stripes too

their eyes are all asking
are you in or are you out
and I think, oh man
what is this about . . .

i just want to show you
the way that i feel . . .

(from *In Or Out*, 1992)

"The queer community has been fighting for so long for an open, inclusive acceptance of indifference," Ani told *The Advocate*. "They know it's not just black and white. These socially constructed divisions can be overly simplistic and claustrophobic, at least speaking for myself. I've always had pressure on both sides 'Hey, stake a flag, right here — where are you going to be?' But it's not something I can choose. I don't experience love or sex as sleeping with a woman or a man. It's a person. It does seem, though, that the music industry has given some special currency to women who come out as lesbians that it doesn't give to male stars who are sexually ambiguous like, say (R.E.M.'s) Michael Stipe."

"I think our ability and our right to identify ourselves is really important," Ani told Emily Lloyd during a 1994 interview for *Off Our Backs*. "In any marginalized community, whether people identify themselves or not affects us all. In that sense I think it really is important to say it, to put it in the face of society at large. So, yeah, I guess being closeted was never an option for me. I don't find that useful in any way. When I wrote *In Or Out*, naively my intention was to throw off all labels: 'Don't narrow my options; it's hard enough to find someone to love.' But what happened is that 'bisexual' — the big, inescapable label — came down on my head . . . which is fine, I guess. Being labelled as bisexual can be a drag, though, because you're never quite part of the inner circle. But I'd rather suffer the consequences of truth than of silence. Still, ultimately, I would prefer a world where who I slept with wasn't as important as what I have to say, what I have to offer the world." Polar themes of disillusionment and affirmation which take on the form of art in two 'girl' songs from these two albums, *Not A Pretty Girl* and *Joyful Girl*.

i am not a pretty girl
this is what i do
i ain't no damsel in distress
and i don't need to be rescued . . .
i am not an angry girl
but it seems like i've got everyone fooled
every time i say something
they find hard to hear
they chalk it up to my anger
never to their fear . . .
i have earned my disillusionment
i have been working all my life
i am a patriot
i have been fighting the good fight . . .
i want to be more than a pretty girl.

(from *Not A Pretty Girl*, 1995)

i do it for the joy it brings
because i'm a joyful girl
because the world owes me nothing
and we owe each other the world . . .
everything i do is judged
and they mostly get it wrong
but oh well
'cuz the bathroom mirror has not budged
and the woman who lives there can tell
the truth from the stuff they say
and she looks me in the eye
and says would you prefer the easy way
no, well o.k. then
don't cry . . .
and i do it just because i want to
because i want to

(from *Joyful Girl*, 1996)

The steady stream of touring during these years left little time for intense relationships or consolation. "It's kind of lonely. I mean, I like my job," Ani told *Monkey Magnet* in 1995. "There's a lot of people that I touch base with all over, but then again I don't have the opportunity to spend much time with any of them. . . . It's just one of those sacrifices you make."

Media attention began to focus on Ani's relative successes. Interviews and stories began talking about her business-woman savvy, her DIY ethics, her growing fan base and touring attendances, as in the November 1996 edition of *CNNfn*: "In six years it (Righteous Babe Records) has evolved from a living-room and car-trunk operation into a viable independent label with an office, eight full-time employees, distribution arrangements around the world and catalog sales exceeding 500,000. . . . DiFranco admitted that she did pay a cost by going the independent route, saying she could have gained the exposure she has now in six months with a major label instead of the 10 years it took on her own. But, she added, 'if you have 10 years and you enjoy what you're doing, it's possible.' She's also making money. DiFranco sold 260,000 units this year, which is impressive for an independent label artist. She also does well on the road with a touring profit margin of 25 percent. She usually sells out more than 100 shows a year. . . . 'Anybody now who has misgivings about their record company or who are starting out and thinking of remaining independent, come to us,' she said."

And with the success of DILATE, the press waxed philosophical about a "movement" of female singer-songwriters with Ani at the forefront of the pack (alongside Alanis Morissette). "Ani DiFranco's eighth album is a study in contrasts," *CMJ*'s Megan Frampton wrote in 1996. "Her self-possession and songwriting are as confident as ever, although her lyrics, conversely, paint her as alone and helpless. . . . Although it is inevitable that DiFranco will get compared to Alanis Morissette . . . DiFranco has made the mold for Morissette to follow in, rather than the other way around. . . . DILATE's 11 songs of love and pain are as personal as reading a diary." However, Ani was not comfortable in this media and fan assigned role as leader of a movement, being a long-time non-conformist herself. "A lot of people come to the shows and listen to the albums and get something out of them," Ani told *Ms.* in 1996. "And that's cool. They're fine. It's the crazy people, the angry people that I come into contact with, the really fervent ones who are up front, and the really crazy ones who are at the backstage bus or at the door of the hotel. I want to think they're only a small percentage of the fans, but of course it seems like they're all fucking crazy and they're making me miserable. I'm standing there singing and there are young girls screaming, five feet from me — screaming in my face the whole time. I turn on late-night TV in hotel rooms all over America, and I see TV evangelists and people testifying — their eyes are rolling back and they're falling over, they're flailing. Then I step on stage and I see the same thing, because people are people — people have those same tendencies. It doesn't matter if you're a little baby dyke in an urban setting or someone else in a rural setting. People have those same tendencies." Tendencies she brought to her music in the lyrics for *Superhero* on the DILATE album.

sleep walking through the all-nite drugstore
baptized in fluorescent light
i found religion in the greeting card aisle
now i know Hallmark was right
and every pop song on the radio
is suddenly speaking to me
art may imitate life
but life imitates tv . . .

i used to be a superhero
no one could touch me
not even myself
you are like a phone booth
that i somehow stumbled into
and now look at me
i am just like everybody else . . .

(from *Superhero*, 1996)

In July 1996, Ani traveled to Ireland to perform at the Galway Arts Festival, followed by dates in Wales, Reading (for WOMAD), London. Then it was on to Germany, Switzerland, Italy, and Belgium. Her first trips to France and Norway occurred in late 1996. 1996 also saw her first appearance on *NBC's Late Nite With Conan O'Brien* television show.

By 1996, Ani had become one of the 50 top grossing concert draws in the U.S. The U.S. dates on her 1996 tour were the sources of inspiration for Ani's double CD LIVING IN CLIP live set (released in 1997). From locales as "exotic" as Spokane (Washington), Arcafa (California), Eugene (Oregon) and more, the live album became a favorite of fans. Many called it the definitive Ani statement, and her love of live performance was evident thanks to superb concert renditions. D.M Avery's 1997 *CMJ* review of the album states, "None of DiFranco's albums have successfully captured her high-energy performances, her musicianly rapport with bassist Sara Lee and drummer Andy Stochansky, her devoted fans' reaction, or her adorable stage banter — until now." Ani's notes show insight into how her tours worked. On her liner noters for LIVING IN CLIP, she wrote: "These recordings represent a handful of the suspect situations (orchestra, anyone?) and ludicrous venues that I followed my guitar into, in the past year . . . baroque, sculpted theaters and dark, skanky rock clubs, hockey stadiums and airplane hangars, tents, balloons and sweaty basement bars where I could smell the audience (and vice versa, God forbid)." The orchestral sessions came as a result of performances held during the inauguration of Buffalo's new hockey stadium. The title of the album came from the term sound engineers used to describe the VU meter of a console being continually in "the red" or "clipping."

In 1998 Ani visited the Netherlands, Spain, and Japan with return visits to Italy (where her recordings were finally released domestically) and Australia. On March 27th, Ani appeared on David Letterman's *Late Night Show*. Later that year saw an appearance on VH1's *Hard Rock Live Show*. While she was still performing at the occasional folk festival, DiFranco was now getting bookings in 3,000 to 20,000 seater auditoriums, concert halls, or clubs, organized by Fleming/Tamulevich, who also handle artists as musically diverse as Mary Lou Lord, Dar Williams, Blue Rodeo, and Great Big Sea.

A series of soundtrack inclusions, guest appearances on compilation albums, and television appearances saw her become the attention of more media scrutiny as reporters from CNN, the major music and lifestyle magazines, underground and alternative presses, *Forbes* and *Ms.* magazines (who praised her "corporate savvy") all begged for interviews. Ani, in her own inimitable way, found the attention flattering, but ill-fitting. Many of the projects Ani chose to be involved with came about because of something *personal*. Like her involvement in *Steal This Movie (Abbie!)*, an indie project about the life of the activist Abbie Hoffman directed by Robert Greenwald. "My daughters think DiFranco walks on water and convinced me to listen," Greenwald commented. "She's perfect for this film, as she is the heir to the likes of Woody Guthrie or Phil Ochs." Ani was commissioned to cover some '60s songs and underscore the biopic. Her compilation appearances have all been for worthy causes (protecting natural habitats, prison reform, women's rights).

With the release of LITTLE PLASTIC CASTLE in early 1998, Ani had settled into a standard tour/release/tour/release groove. The album benefitted from having the presence of Ani's live band on most of the album's cuts. That sense of family helped make the songs sound deeper and richer than on previous albums. *All Music Guide* critic Darryl Carter wrote of LITTLE PLASTIC CASTLE: "She released this record after spending a year promoting her first live CD by repeatedly admitting to reporters that her studio albums lack the vitality of her concert performances. Rock critics agreed *en masse*, and their praise for the live album helped propel DiFranco to a new level of mainstream stardom. . . . Her excellent band had plenty of time to gel on the road, and their performances here are as tight, driven and intense as they've ever been. . . . This is the most creatively produced DiFranco album to date, combining her distinctly frenetic acoustic fingerstyle with computer samples, dance rhythms, Mariachi brass and full-band rock jams. The result is colorful — almost cartoony — but almost never overshadows the emotional content." Kim Hughes in *Now Magazine* had a somewhat different take on this CD, however: "Fans aren't still stewing over what's been printed about Ani DiFranco, so why is she? You'd think after having opened for Bob Dylan and closed for thousands more around the world, DiFranco would just get over it instead of lashing out at the 'girl police' who view wearing lipstick as an act of treason against feminism. But there she is, bitterly howling at her detractors right in the first song on LITTLE PLASTIC CASTLE. The government and one-dimensional radio stations are the next to get the boot. Once the perspective turns personal, things improve, with

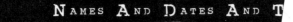

songs like *Deep Dish* offering a bouncy melodicisr
been DiFranco's calling card but that suits her su
smile, baby, you're massive. Besides, it's not a si
fans sing along."

Ani's use of Kingsway Studios in New Orleans led to a love of
city's music which manifested itself openly when she hired The Rebirth
Brass Band to be her opening act for the LITTLE PLASTIC CASTLE
Tour. "That place is a petri dish for indigenous music," Ani told the
San Francisco Chronicle in 1998. "The brass bands came from the African
American community. There are many, many of these folk scenes brewing
beneath the veneer of pop culture, and they're the ones making the real
alternative music."

The ultimate badge of mass media acceptance, it must have seemed
to Ani, was being nominated for a Grammy Award in 1997 for the 1998
ceremony. *Shy*, as performed by Ani on LIVING IN CLIP, was nominated for
the prestigious NARAS (National Academy of Recording Arts and
Sciences) statuette in the Female Rock Performance category. Though
she didn't win, most of her fans must have thought that Ani had, finally,
"made it big."

KNOW NOW THEN

What's known of Ani's private life during these years, beyond what she
reveals in her lyrics? (Ani would be the first to ask, "What private life?").
Well, she's close friends with Indigo Girl Amy Ray. "She's a doll," Ani said
of Ray in a March 1998 article from *Diva* magazine by Lucy O'Brien titled
"Power Babe." "I love her dearly. We're very similar in lots of ways. We're
both in the position of being pseudo-rock stars but neither of us is
impressed with the whole thing. We call each other up every couple of
weeks and bring each other back down to earth." Both met on tour and
share tattoos they've had done by Joan Jett's tattoo artist in New York
City. The two of them have often talked of forming an all-"chick" folksinger revue a-la Lilith Fair and calling it The Rolling Thunder Pussy
Revue (an obvious salute to Bob Dylan's classic concerts of the 1970s).
That said, Ani is rather nonplussed by Lilith Fair, the Sarah McLachlan

...ganized festival celebrating womanhood in all its myriad musical styles. It isn't so much that Ani doesn't like the idea, she just feels there should be nothing unusual about a bunch of women getting together to sing songs about what being a woman is like. What would her tour be like? "I'd love to get Oumou Sangare (whose latest release is titled MOUSSOLOU on World Circuit — RQ), this amazing West African singer/violinist," Ani told *Spin* in its May 1998 issue, "and Tribe 8, Lucinda Williams, Salt-N-Pepa (they rock so hard), Mary Margaret O'Hara, Queen Latifah. Boy, now I'm pipe dreaming. We were talking about having a house band with different women fronting it. Can you imagine a revolving door on the mike, with Me'Shell Ndegeocello on bass, Bonnie Raitt on guitar, Sheila E. on drums? Fuck, I'd be creaming!"

Of her tattoos, Ani calls them her life's scars, "pictures of places I've been," as she told Lucy O'Brien in the February-March 1998 issue of *Diva*. "They're mile markers, road maps, pictures of places I've been to." They remain testimonies to her sense of who she is and what she's all about. Her most prominent one appears on her collarbone, a symmetrically designed set of lines evoking (abstractly) the image of a bird in flight. A smaller version of the tattoo appears at the nape of her neck.

Ani is keenly aware of her own sense of fashion and flaunts styles openly and irreverently. Her chameleon-like, shape-shifting appearance changes very often and covers hair style and color as well as clothing. At various incarnations along her road to stardom, her hair has been every color under the rainbow and every length conceivable. Nowadays, her hair has remained short and somewhat wavy with just a hint of a white streak. For the most part, the diminutive performer (she's only 5'2") sports chunky-heeled boots and wears rather conservative make-up. But she's been known to sport a variety of 'dos and facial styles, given her mood and the circumstance. The sense of anti-fashion as fashion comes both from her formative years and from not wanting to portray a fixed image. Her hairstyle changes have been credited to her insomnia, the result of after-performance jitters and "second winds" that leave her awake until 3 or 4 a.m. Fans meeting her after shows may be somewhat intrigued by her nails, a combination of press-on nails and electrical tape. She uses them as picks and seem the logical things to use given her sharp, pointed, almost percussive style of playing. "My claws," she called them in a December

1994 article in *Guitar Player* penned by James Rotondi. "I can slam and pull so hard. My guitars are always in the shop. I knock the braces out of the insides. I've even got to tape the pick up and the battery down."

Ani's been quoted as having had two lesbian relationships which deeply moved her. In 1997, Ani told *The Advocate*, "Right now, being in a couple, I do really miss the babes in my life. The women friends in my life — they've been missing for a long time. There are a few people in my life — one in particular — we've seen each other very briefly in the last year a couple of times. We had some problems and, you know, it's not time right now." To this day, she remains friends with both women, admitting that she felt a deeper bond with them than with any male relationships she had up to meeting Andy Gilchrist. Her romance with Gilchrist stems from their shared experiences on the road, in the studio and outside of the music they make together. "He's so kind to me, he's so funny, we have so much fun, and we get each other through all this shit," Ani told Achy Obejas. Her lesbian experiences notwithstanding, Ani never openly called herself "queer," choosing instead to refer to her sexual orientation as "ambivalent."

In 1996, Ani drove her VW beetle down to Austin Texas to record THE PAST DIDN'T GO ANYWHERE, her collaboration with Utah Phillips. The relationship seemed mutual with both singers admiring the other greatly. Their friendship remains a deeply moving one for Ani who admires Phillips' steadfastness in the face of big money, big business, big government and big "idiocy." Ani's music and production for THE PAST DIDN'T GO ANYWHERE brought his vignettes to life for a younger generation who had never heard of Phillips (or most of the events the man retold for that matter). "Utah is such a wonderful teacher when it comes to American history," Ani told *Mother Jones* magazine, "so I've certainly learned a lot of things from him and our friendship along the way. . . . We share a booking agent and we were both staying at some doctor's house one night many years ago, back in folk music's sleep-on-somebody's-couch days." Phillips sent Ani performance tapes. Spoken words were selected, music was added. "I started to take things he said between songs and try them over music I was making and I just improvised a bunch of music to sort of put a sonic landscape behind his stories. . . . I think anybody who has the opportunity to hear Utah will pretty much respond on some level. I think it's all a matter of what you're exposed to. If you turn on the TV, you're going to get a certain palate, and if you go looking underneath the surface, there's a whole lot of stuff there that I think a lot of our generation would be really interested in." Reviewers were thrilled. In *Addicted To Noise*, the reviewer wrote, "Through the timeless practice of spinning a yarn and shuffling its established structure with technology, DiFranco has painted an innovative portrait of a classic American artist. With Ani undeniably at the helm, Utah has been made accessible to the masses in spite of himself." "A truly inspired project," stated *No Depression*, in its March-May 1997 issue. "She's from Generation-X, he from much earlier in the alphabet, and together they've taken a newfangled approach to closing the age-old gap. . . . This rap-and-rhythm collaboration is truly hip-hop — as in 'hypnotic' and 'hopeful.'"

Sometime in 1996-1997, Ani bought a modern two-story house in a downtown block in Buffalo where her and her mother reside. Elizabeth continues to stand by her daughter and works for Righteous Babe Records as well. By bringing it all back home, Ani felt a certain amount of control, more so than she could have had she remained in New York City. Besides, it was a great opportunity to give something back to her "rust-belt" home town. "To have a good job in Buffalo is something rare. To be able to give people jobs is a great feeling," Ani told *The New York Times* in 1998.

In 1997, at age twenty-six, Ani got to meet and perform on the same stage as Bob Dylan. And if outsiders believed that Ani would have fallen in a swoon finding herself in the same presence as Unca Bob, the 'Voicebox of His Generation', then they would be surprised to learn that Ani had heard of him, certainly heard most of his songs, but only really liked OH MERCY, Dylan's 1989 collaboration with U2 producer and Hamilton, Ontario native Daniel Lanois. At a performance in New Jersey, *Addicted To Noise*'s Frank Tortorici reported on Ani's sway over uninitiated Dylan fans who reacted favorably to "her every turn of the phrase."

Ani's first real turn as a record producer came when Sony's Work imprint released Dan Bern's 50 EGGS. Like Ani, Bern had navigated folk circles and had seen his DIY recordings lead him into a college/university setting. 50 EGGS was Bern's second release for Sony and it was filled with trademark wit and sardonicism. Ani-alumni Jason Mercer, Sara Lee, and Andy Stochansky lent musical support, as did Ani whose production gives the artist room to maneuver. Ani's occasional musical contributions add color and shading. In an April 1998 article from *Addicted To Noise*, Ani stated, "Dan is a kick-ass songmaker. Anyone who cares a lot about good songwriting is gonna like this album. . . . Dan is one of the most dynamic and engaging songwriters I've ever known." Ani's luck must have rubbed off, for the album charted decently and attracted good reviews and press despite no real radio exposure. It proved to be a very different experience than her production of a track on Janis Ian's THE HUNGER the year before. Ian, a veritable symbol of the heart-on-sleeve type of songwriter so prevalent in the 1970s, had asked Ani to produce the album. "I was very busy and didn't have a lot of time," Ani told *Diva*, "so I said, 'Let's do one song.' We spent three days in the studio recording the song. Then I mixed it and gave it to her. I was kinda disappointed when I heard the final product, because she had taken out all the low end. It was like, 'Oh my God, not my sound at all.' It had come down to a vocal, snare, a little guitar and phut! It had started as such a heavy tune with a beautiful bass line going through it. The essence of the tune to me was the endless groove. But then, I guess you should just let it go, because it's her album."

In May 1998, a decidedly Ani DiFranco-esque character appeared sporting Ani's voice on the Fox-TV animated series *King of the Hill*. The popular adult-animation series (created by *Beavis & Butthead*'s Mike Judge) featured DiFranco as Emily, a feminist rock and roller who tries to dissuade main character Peggy Hill from being a typical little housewife. Judge's artist gave Emily avocado green hair, a nose ring, and a decidedly DiFranco look. The show also featured Willie Nelson, Green Day, and the late Tammy Wynette. "That was excellent," Ani told the *San Francisco Chronicle*. "I'm an animated person anyway. I've felt like a cartoon my whole life. The script explored different communities of women, and one wifey's inner desire for liberation. It's about being wed to heterosexual hegemony and a — husband. But hey, we should all be allowed our individual brands of psychosis."

On June 2, 1998, MTV announced Ani had married Andrew Gilchrist during a private ceremony. The wedding caught the media unawares. But, in all honesty, her relationship with her drummer "Goat Boy" (Gilchrist's nickname) had been evident in interviews and intimated — at least to the ears of some fans — on DILATE. The two had fallen in love in 1995 and had kept the relationship relatively quiet. "[He's] really extreme," Ani told *The Advocate*. "He's so kind to me, he's so funny, we have so much fun, and we get each other through all this shit. I couldn't have premeditated this. People have to put up with me and my big mouth always telling my side of the story — plus the whole public noose around my neck the whole time. He's really good at dealing with it; he doesn't give a fuck. He keeps me sane." Her marriage to Andy Gilchrist continues amid the roar and clatter of gay and lesbian individuals who believe she's somehow "betrayed" them.

On September 19, 1998, Ani appeared on stage with Me'Shell Ndegeocello, Amerindian poet/rocker John Trudell (whose Rykodisc releases are fully recommended and endorsed by the author), and Michael Franti (Spearhead and Disposable Heroes Of Hiphoprisy) at the Berkeley Community Theater in Berkeley, California for a benefit in support of the state's Coalition for Women Prisoners and the Prison Activist Resource Center. It was yet another benefit in support of a cause Ani strongly believes in, the reform of the schooling infrastructure to prevent young people from resorting to a life of crime. "The whole criminal justice system really gets my goat," Ani told *Girlfriends* magazine in 1999. "I've been involved for a bunch of years with these issues. The existence of the death penalty is one of the most reprehensible things in our country. We have a culture of imprisonment as an alternative to education and basic employment. It's how our government deals with what it views as an expandable population. Plus doing the benefit gave me the chance to work with Angela Davis who's a hero to my stompy booted feminist chick."

The album UP UP UP UP UP UP (which I'll call UPX6 from here on in) was released in January 1999, her fourteenth release for RBR and her tenth album of original material. While the album didn't chart as spectacularly as LITTLE PLASTIC CASTLE (it did debut at a respectable number 29 on *Billboard*'s Top 200 Charts) or earn the same kind of rave reviews, fans quickly made it one of their faves. In a RBR press release interview, Ani expanded on the process by which UPX6 came about. "This album was recorded on sixteen tracks (or less) of ADAT and very little effects were used at all, seriously, not even reverbs. The sound of the vocals on *Angel Food* are me singing through a bullet mike into a guitar amp. The whole album was tracked live with a few overdubs. It basically is the sound of the band playing live in the studio, relating to our surroundings and utilizing the various mikes, amps, and rooms available. There's no need to go out of your way to be uncreative in the studio, but creativity doesn't just mean gear, either. Live on stage your tools are limited by circumstance: one room sound, one microphone to sing into, maybe a coupla guitars but at Kingsway (Studio in New Orleans), for instance, the possibilities are endless. We set up all over the house and played with the instruments and toys we found there. I was experimenting mostly prior to the sound hitting the tape, not after." How did UPX6 differ from previous releases? "DILATE is sorta unique in its concentrated, emotional, first-person-ality and LPC contains a lot of observations about my job and my life in the lengthened shadow of public possession and media misrepresentation but now that the tortured relationship of DILATE dun got fixed, and I've stopped reading or being aware of any press, chatter or opinion of me whatsoever, my writing is back to business as usual, I suppose. It's not so much a stepping away, as a return." The album saw Ani being far more playful (musically speaking) thanks to a fatter bottom and some trip hop/dance-groove effects. One track, *Hat Shaped Hat*, was edited down to thirteen minutes from a three-hour jam, which RBR describes as being "right at home on some great lost Funkadelic album."

Some critics didn't quite see it that way. Tim Perlich of *Now Magazine* wrote, with a fashionable cynicism, "Perhaps tired from shouldering the problems of the human race, Ani DiFranco sounds beat on most of the decidedly down-spirited UPX6, her once feisty shout reduced to a sleepy croak. It's entirely possible that she recorded all her observations of everyday social injustice while reclining on a futon. Aside from the obvious Starbucks and Borders in-store play appeal of the quieter, gentler, unobtrusive approach, the new recordings also indicate the real possibility of performing her entire tour from a horizontal position. Many long-time fans who survived the lipstick shock may find the mildly morose Ani to be a poor substitute to the angry Ani of old." Becky Byrkit of AMG wrote, "The self-appointed CEO of intrepid indie grrl-rock sparks one more with UPX6, an ebullient addition to an already prolific and deeply admirable career. The playful synthetics and occasional stabs at atypical DiFranco stylings belie the general humorlessness of her lyrics. . . . Some fans may continue to dream of an album wherein Ani shows off some real chops, as she'll do for lucky people in concert — she's actually a wonderful 12-string guitarist, but you can't really get a feel for that here." But *People* magazine's Steve Dougherty said, "DiFranco creates a spare, mesmerizing batch of treats, including *'Tis Of Thee*, about an America that forgets its poor and is transfixed by Jerry Springer; *Trickle Down*, set in the streets of Buffalo; and a gospel inflected ditty in which she scat-sings about an all-night rap session with 'a man in the shape of a man/holding a hat-shaped hat.'" Q Magazine's Paul Davies wrote, "One more passionate and powerful release from the Buffalo, NY singer-songwriter. Transparently fired by the roots and traditions of folk music, Ani DiFranco's stridently unambiguous and beautiful voice hitches the acoustic trappings of her muse to a maverick indie sensibility. There is fragility here, but it's tempered with a toughness and feisty resilience which belies her relative youth."

The album also included Ani's coming-to-terms-with-her-parents song, *Angry Anymore*, a gentle and wise closing to this part of her life.

growing up it was just me and my mom
against the world
and all my sympathies were with her
when i as a little girl
but now i've seen both my parents
play out the hands they were dealt
and as each year goes by
i know more about what my father must have felt

i just want you to understand
that i know what all the fighting was for
and i just want you to understand
that i'm not angry anymore
i'm not angry anymore

she taught me how to wage a cold war
with quiet charm
but i just want to walk
through my life unarmed
to accept and just get by

like my father learned to do
but without all the acceptance and getting by
that got my father through . . .

(from *Angry Anymore*, 1999)

During 1999 Ani appeared on PBS's *The Mississippi: River of Song* mini-series as narrator and was selected as a jurist in the John Lennon Songwriting Contest. In April she appeared at the first People's Poetry Festival in New York City. The event was a three-day symposium of writers and performers celebrating the joy of poetry as an oral tradition. Through lectures, workshops, discussions, and performances, a diverse array of artists, writers, and performers participated. Guests included Robert Bly (the father of the so-called Men's Movement), John Trudell, poet Robert Pinsky, and Ani. Nicole Volk, reporting for *Music Blvd*, commented that "At her Sunday (April 11) afternoon show at Cooper Union's Great Hall, she performed more spoken word than songs and thrilled the sold-out crowd with her half-hour set. She emerged in a Yankees t-shirt and paid homage to her former poetry teacher Sekou Sundiata, who opened the show. 'If there's anybody who taught me what I know, it's that guy.' In light of the Kosovo bombings, she read *Not So Soft*. Later she quipped, 'It's such a strange thing to be standing here without a guitar. My midriff feels so exposed . . .' DiFranco also read some of her work from LITTLE PLASTIC CASTLE, including *Pulse* and *Fuel*, before finally picking up a guitar to play *Independence Day*. She exited to another standing ovation." Her performance at Washington Irving High School that same evening had Utah Phillips opening the show and a playful Ani joking about how much she enjoyed Suzanne Somers' poetry and how much she missed New York City. Nicole Volk continued to say, "When one fan screamed 'Fuck Giuliani!' DiFranco said that when she first heard that at a show, she didn't know it was a reference to New York's mayor and she and her keyboard player Julie (Wolf) thought it was a lewd suggestion to what DiFranco ought to do to her. 'We had to have that explained to us!' A fan's plea for a cover of Britney Spears was met with one of DiFranco's own songs, woven with bits of *Amazing Grace* and the Sugarhill Gang's *Rapper's Delight* instead."

_y 1999, Ani's second collaborative effort with folk singer/ activist/grandpa-with-a-punk-attitude Utah (nee Bruce) Phillips appeared on store shelves. While it didn't chart, it did earn more praise, thanks to a "live-in-the-studio" feel. FELLOW WORKERS featured DiFranco and friends supporting Phillips on more political rants, non-history-book history lessons on the dark underbelly of American labor circa the turn of the 20th century, and ruminations about life in general. The material had been recorded at Kingsway Studios in New Orleans in December 1998. Soul Asylum's Dave Pirner appeared on trumpet on a track. The release was Phillips idea, Ani explains in a press release: "Utah proposed to me the idea of creating a second record together. . . . So . . . you know me . . . I can never resist a challenge, and FELLOW WORKERS looked to me like a crazy opportunity for Utah and I to attempt a kind of collaboration that was entirely new to us both." Of the recording session itself, Keith Spera, reporting for the New Orleans *Times-Picayune*, stated, "DiFranco and her band managed the delicate task of supplying accompaniment that had its own integrity, but did not overwhelm Phillips. . . . Judging from his satisfied grin and knowing nods, Phillips approved of their efforts." Phillips himself stated in an RBR press release interview, "Ani invited me and my son Brendan to New Orleans to sing with her tribe in front of live people while being recorded. When we were done, I walked away from it, trusting Ani's judgment to do the right thing. She did. I didn't know what this recording was going to sound like until it showed up in the mail. Bingo!"

Summer 1999 saw Ani embark on a 25-date tour of North America with former James Brown saxophonist Maceo Parker (whose Verve albums, especially LIFE ON PLANET GROOVE, have been favorites of Ani's) as opening act, billed in RBR press releases as the "Funk and Folk" or the "F-Word Tour," where the "Mistress of Folk meets the Master of Funk." "I think I've seen Maceo live more than anyone else," Ani stated in her press release for the event. "He's one of my ultimate heroes . . . he's just amazing." The concerts also featured the "skills of a pair of acclaimed female DJs for some free-style frenzy at each show," the RBR press release declared. DJ Courtney took on the task for the first half the tour, while DJ Tamara handled the closing half. Toronto fans at the Molson Amphitheatre were privy to a superb show filled with dancing, swaying and a sing-a-long like atmosphere that earned high marks from fans and reviewers alike. Fans were treated to old faves, new songs, and the usual bizarro mix of Ani cover tunes like The Artist's *When Doves Cry*, Rick James' *Super Freak*, Woody Guthrie's *Do Re Mi*, and Stevie Wonder's *I Wish*.

On the heels of the F Word tour, Buffalo fans were eagerly awaiting an October concert date with the Buffalo Philharmonic. Unforseen circumstances forced the show to be rescheduled at some point in the new year, however. Internet sources speculate the show will be held at some point in the first week of June 2000. Fall 1999 saw the release of two non-Ani related releases on Righteous Babe Records. The first was an album of spoken word recordings by Sekou Sundiata, Ani's New School for Social Research professor and mentor. Sundiata had previously released an album (THE BLUE ONENESS OF DREAMS). "He's an amazing person," Ani told *Billboard*'s Melinda Newman in the July 3, 1999 issue. "He's got such a beautiful presence and is such a poetic being; he's a big hero of mine." RBR plans on publishing a companion book of Sundiata's poetry based on the recording, another first for the company. RBR's second non-Ani album is a new release, PRIZE, by Brazilian/American avant-garde musician Arto Lindsay. Ani met the influential and critically revered artist while in New York. A backstage discussion led to her finding out that Lindsay was shopping for a new label deal. Ani and Scot dove right in. If both releases don't sound like they'll amount to much outside of critical circles, both show how passionate Ani is about what she's doing with RBR. While Ani continues to perform across North America, she'll be working on her Woody Guthrie tribute which is planned for RBR release at some time in the new year. Already, a number of high-profile guests have signed on. The project has been in the works for a couple of years and, in true DiFranco fashion, is being handled the way she wants it to be handled.

During the summer Ani had somehow found the time to participate on The Artist's new release (titled RAVE UN2 THE JOY FANTASTIC on Arista/NPG) — and to complete TO THE TEETH, her most recent recording, for which the press release from Tracy Mann at The Press Network (Ani's publicist) reads: "Ani DiFranco explores a world armed TO THE TEETH on her latest album. . . . It's never been a secret that Ani DiFranco is a dizzyingly prolific songwriter. After all, we're talking about a musician with more than a hundred songs under her belt by the time she reached her twentieth birthday — and that was fourteen records ago. With brazen disregard for music industry convention, the Little Folksinger now releases her third album of 1999 alone. Hot on the heels of UP UP UP UP UP UP and FELLOW WORKERS . . . TO THE TEETH sends 13 brand-new tunes into orbit, carried aloft by Ani's trademark combo of political and personal insight, vocal fireworks, high-velocity fingerwork and funkalicious grooves. Ani plays lots o' instruments here, including guitars of every stripe, of course, but also bass, drums, piano, organ, even megaphone and banjo. . . . Ani herself is the first to admit that TO THE TEETH is different from any of her previous albums, 'in the sense that it spans a year of various recording situations; it brings together a bunch of different studio settings for me.' . . . While several of the songs were written and performed during the summer '99 F-Word Tour, plenty of them have not yet been heard by anyone, anywhere. 'For me one of the most exciting things was having a couple of my musical heroes on the record,' Ani says. Sure enough, legendary James Brown/George Clinton sideman (and F-Word Tour special guest) Maceo Parker is on hand on tenor sax and flute, plus another feller whose name might ring a bell: The Artist Formerly Known As Prince, who, in DiFranco's words, 'sang the shit out of *Providence*'. There's no question that even long-time Ani aficionados will find still more stunning surprises here. . . . As always, Ani's latest songs ring with the urgency of newspaper headlines and the intimacy of journal entries. The latest round of gun-related violence inspired the title track, while *Hello Birmingham,* is a poignant take on the murder of Dr. Barnett Slepian at the hands of an opponent to abortion rights in Ani's home town. From these wrenching accounts of American life at the end of the century to the simple joys of watching lovers reunite at *The Arrivals Gate*, TO THE TEETH is proof positive that, as a songwriter, musician and producer, Ani DiFranco continues to defy all guesses as to where she's going next." Her achievement in 1999 was recognized with two Grammy Award nominations: *Jukebox* from UPX6 earned a nomination for the Female Rock Vocal Performance and the album FELLOW WORKERS for Best Contemporary Folk Recording.

The future may bring more changes, more adventures, more discoveries. But one thing is certain: whatever road Ani takes, it won't be the most boring one.

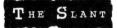

The Slant

i am a work in progress
dressed in the fabric
of a world unfolding
offering me intricate
patterns of questions . . .

(from The Slant)

SHE SAYS

Them's the facts, but what's the slant, as Ani might say? What's the skinny? The 411? What's herstory? What does she believe? What makes her mind tick? It's righteousness, babe. And when you come across someone as opinionated as Ani, chances are you're going to run across things she's been quoted as saying and think, "God, how forthright! I wish I'd said that!" Righteousness feels good. As for self-righteousness, Ani pulls back at the brink of this abyss every time, though some of her fans may not.

So here we are, a new millennium staring at us in the face like the Emerald City before Dorothy, Toto, the Scarecrow, the Tin Woodsman, and the Cowardly Lion. It's a scary, bold new world where kids can take guns into high schools and shoot their peers and teachers just because they feel like it, not for any cause, righteous or not. What's right and what's wrong, behaving justly, righteous thought and conduct — these qualities of life seem to be more and more ephemeral every day. And, it seems, few people care.

So Ani says as she sings of the complacency of the individual faced with the chronic woes of a world that understands nothing and wants everything. Where consumers are told to drink the "dog coffee" that's handed down to them without question. Where the "government" controls the image, controls the level at which everyday people are manipulated into thinking their consumerism means they look like the "haves" when they still squarely belong to the "have-nots." Ani's songs sing of the power and vision of individuals doggedly clinging to their individuality in the face of politics: whether they're the politics of the bedroom, the boardroom, the "I'm oh so bored room." She is a champion of these small voices. As she was quoted in the *San Francisco Chronicle*, "if you're not angry, you're numb, ignorant or apathetic. . . . I have a tremendous amount of hope, otherwise I wouldn't be putting so much energy into this. The hardest thing is for people to hear that if you want things to be different, it takes you getting out there and actually doing something. A very small minority of people are doing things, while the opinion of the vast majority goes unspoken. I don't believe that what is going on now is the world any of us wants to live in."

Throughout her career as a singer, a chronicler of woes, a DIY troubadour, Ani has always believed that the individual has power to make changes. Sure, one lone voice in the wilderness might sound like a pitiful cry while facing that horde of lemmings heading out to sea, but sing loud and hard and true enough, and you get others to look up, up, up, up, up, up — to ask the one question governments (and banks and record companies and other corporations) don't want to hear.

"Why?"

It's the tug and pull of the quotidian that creates the pathos of our existences. Most of us give in to the material side of life at the expense of the spiritual (thereby allowing those who peddle the material side of spirituality to make a living and profit, too). Faced with a burden of shrinking personal wealth before the enormous cost of living a decent life, most of us cave in to consumerism. Trying to stay true to dreams and visions, most of us abandon them early on, settling for the 2.5 kids and the white picket fence without ever once stepping into the great beyond in search of adventure and discovery. Righteousness very rarely enters into it, unless giving the finger to the guy suffering from road rage who just passed you on a double solid yellow line counts.

The one constant theme throughout her career has been Ani's quest for the control of her own destiny in the face of people who would manipulate her image to satisfy their desire for possession or gain. As she says in an interview in *Spin*, "If I look at myself as a teenager now, I just fucking hate the kind of girl I was. You know, spineless and ridiculous and totally manipulatable. But I don't take shit now!" The dynamic of this quest is the tug and pull of artifice versus creativity, manufactured image versus sincere content, trend versus personality, cool reason versus passionate abandon, community pressure versus personal fulfilment. The desire for justice in a seemingly unjust world. The worse thing that could happen, especially if you're Ani DiFranco, is to give up the struggle, to be swallowed by the unthinking whole, succumbing to the suits who would have you wear PVC leather skirts while walking into the breast augmentation clinic (as filmed by *Entertainment Tonight*). This informs much of what Ani has to say about living in our age.

Mention the corporate world of modern pop music and Ani has a great deal to say. For all of her recorded life, Ani has been at odds with the way the recording industry (man)handles the artist day-to-day. The performer is out there, singing before audiences that may or may not like her, plugging a given album on the interview/promotions tour, recording when and where able, then somehow supposedly finding the time to write songs and have the time for doing the little things that make up a life. All this for the good of the company. Early on, thanks to sure and exceptional advice from people in her life that didn't want her to be chewed up and spat out by the Starmaker Machinery, Ani decided to go it alone. Admittedly, this was done after initial attempts to sell her demos to major record labels had failed. When the majors finally came a-knockin', Ani made sure she wasn't home. Smaller labels proved just as infuriating and unremarkable. To the young Ani, the woman who had studied art and ballet, music and culture, it seemed far more rewarding to enjoy the fruits of your own labor in your own way and on your own terms than to obey The Bottom Line. "I think the music industry, for instance, is such a huge, multibazillion-dollar industry and it's become very, very savvy," Ani says in *Mother Jones*. "There's a very short grace period in which actual human rebellion or resistance can thrive before it's co-opted by these huge companies. And all of youth culture is packaged and sold back to us at this furious rate these days. I think it's part and parcel to this corporate encroachment on our lives in general." In *Newsday*, she says, "I don't think the music industry is conducive to artistic and social change and growth. It does a lot to exploit and homogenize art and artists. In order to challenge the corporate music industry, I feel it necessary to remain outside it . . . I could be selling a lot more albums. Life could be a lot more cushy. But it's much more interesting to try and hammer out an alternative route without the music industry and maybe be an example for other musicians. You don't have to play ball."

And while her recording label often uses the industry's vernacular, its way of promotion and marketing, it isn't bound by any law or practice. Early on, Righteous Babe Records tried to remain a simple operation, and as the success of what Ani was doing took hold, the 'company' grew without sacrificing itself to the majors who would have done anything to buy into that action. If RBR releases promo CDs and offers them to Tower customers who subscribe to the huge record store chain's in-house magazine, then that's OK. It's what is expected. Curiously, however, RBR boasts no web site, opting instead to work with e-mail and the traditional sales routes. At a time when record companies are running scared of Internet downloads and scrambling to maintain their hold over MP3 technology, RBR's caution is unusual and somehow proper, if a trifle old-fashioned, which Ani probably likes to hear.

Indeed, Ani has become somewhat wary of all the attention given to her 'corporate' affairs, as she says in *Mother Jones*: "Having more exposure is kind of a bittersweet thing for me, honestly, because it's nice to have a little more job security in life now. Then there's the down side, having a lot of people who don't really know what I do or what I'm about, but who have formed opinions about me based on what they hear in the media. It can be very frustrating and very deflating to be constantly defined and described by other people, so I've stopped reading anything written about me, and I find it much healthier. I just sort of concentrate on what I do and don't worry too much about that." During a press release interview for UPX6, Ani spoke at length of the problems of running a growing company and still retaining the "little guy" feel. "The monolith that is RBR at this point is funny, and incredible, and scary to me. It's a fascinating position for me to be in here: taking all the credit and all the blame for everything that a disparate semi-independent collection of associated organizations is doing. Flem/Tam books me into a large hall in wheresville ohiowa and folks get mad at me 'cuz I'm not playing small bars any more. Joanna (an RBR staffer) is nice and helpful to someone on the phone and someone somewhere thinks I'm just the coolest and RBR is the shit. My road manager takes it upon himself to decide to turn away a person at the door of a venue, who says they're supposed to have a press pass waiting for them, but doesn't . . . and one outraged writer at the whatsit weekly thinks I'm an asshole. . . . The truth is, I have no idea what goes on at the office most days . . . and one room might not even know what's happening in the next! Mostly, I'm happy to have it grow beyond me and my manager and the trunk of my car and incorporate lots of other people's ideas. I like it that, as the operation grows, the possibilities for getting involved with other people and projects grow. As the platform to speak from becomes more stable, the possibilities for effecting change, providing inspiration, and perpetrating art expand. It's also just damn nice, in life, to have the luxury of surrounding oneself with people who are cool, and interesting, and thoughtful."

Ani has become one of the biggest-selling independent artists on the scene today, and retains control of the publishing rights to her song catalog. Sales of her albums have increased steadily over the course of her ten years in 'da biz'. DILATE, LIVING IN CLIP, LITTLE PLASTIC CASTLE, and UPX6 all charted nationally in the United States. The success of Alana Davis' cover version of *32 Flavors* means she gets paid royalties. Her presence on the best-selling soundtracks to *My Best Friend's Wedding* and *The Jackal* ensure continued promotion to an older audience. While some artists are finding their fan base shrinking, Ani's music continues to be heard by college and university students internationally.

At the start of her DIY career, Ani sold her own cassettes in the back of her car from gig to gig. Placement in indie record stores came next and distribution across a fixed network brought greater exposure of her music to a young audience. Eventually, RBR became an actual company with people employed to do any number of tasks. Today, Righteous Babe's offices are located in a six-story terra-cotta building in Buffalo. Most of the furniture in the building is second hand, bought from closed down businesses in the area. The area itself is largely burnt out, but RBR's presence gives the community a renewed sense of life. Ani had toyed with the idea of relocating RBR to NYC but rejected the idea, remembering her home-town roots and the sad state of business there. Buffalo officials gave her a Common Council Proclamation, and she received star billing at a 1996 gala concert celebrating the new sports arena opening. Her 'backup band' at the event was the Buffalo Philharmonic (two cuts from the show appear on LIVING IN CLIP). RB earns approximately $7.50 on every CD sold at retail. Ani pockets $4.25, almost double what major-label artists receive. RBR claims total catalog sales (to summer of 1999) were two million dollars plus, with sales of LIVING IN CLIP numbering 220,000 copies. Sales for LITTLE PLASTIC CASTLE were quoted at 250,000 copies. Her concerts now generate remarkable revenues. Since 1996, her tours have been ranked among the Top 50 of Top Grossing Tours by Pollstar (peaking at #17 in May/June of 1998). Today, Ani regularly performs to sold-out and almost sold-out shows with seating ranging from between 3,000 and 20,000 seats. A full quarter of concert gross revenues are hers. Much to her credit, Ani re-invests almost everything she makes back into RBR. RBR employees get full benefits and profit sharing. She uses Buffalo companies to manufacture her CDs. Her T-shirts are also screen printed in the Queen City by Planet Love, a company run by former Ani college room-mate Tanya Zabinski and husband Joe DiPasquale, a friend and former construction-business partner of Scot Fisher's. And while the T-shirts she sells at her gigs don't include pictures of her face, they do contain quotes she likes. In each and every respect, Ani and Scot control their business and allow it to grow in their own way and at their own speed. It's been a slow and steady route, one which has brought them greater exposure, better concert receipts, and larger sales margins with each and every release.

But Ani loathes talk about her as a corporate "pioneer," as she said in her open letter to Ms. magazine in response to being named one of 21 women pioneers for the 21st century: "I have indeed sold enough records to open a small office on the half-abandoned main street in the dilapidated urban center of my home town. . . . I am able to hire 15 or so folks to run and constantly reinvent the place while I drive around and play music for people. I am able to give stimulating business to local printers and manufacturers and to employ the services of independent distributors, promoters, booking agents and publicists. I was able to quit my day job and devote myself to what I love. And yes, we are enjoying modest profits these days, affording us the opportunity to reinvest in innumerable political and artistic endeavors. RBR is a vehicle for redefining the relationship between art and commerce in my own life."

Ani's DIY ethos has a long-standing tradition with folk singers, especially those from the women's movement, something she would be quick to acknowledge. One need only look at the career of June Millington (who began performing with Fanny long before the Spice Girls were gleams in their parents' respective eyes) and her Fabulous Records, Olivia Records (founded by a collective of Women performers), one of the premier labels devoted to women's music, Holly Near's founding of The Redwood Music Center (and Redwood Records label), Kate Clinton's Whyscrack Records, Disappear Fear's self-titled label releases, Judy Fjell's Honeypie Records, Susan Herrick's Watchfire Records, and many, many more. The sense of empowerment, of being your own boss, of not having to be undermined by the sheer masculinity of the record industry, is intense and rewarding, infuriating and joyful. Righteous Babe Records is a success because it follows its own path. And although Ani's releases are distributed nationally in the United States by KOCH (in Canada it's Festival, Cooking Vinyl in the U.K., Shock Records in Australia, P-Vine in Japan/Asia, Helicon in Israel), small, independent Women's Music distributors like Zango, Goldenrod, and Ladyslipper still retain distribution rights to her recordings because Ani has protected their right to do so.

Ani's role in the women's movement in contemporary music has placed her at the center of controversy. Mention the whole Spice Girls 'girl power' thing, for example, and Ani bristles with opinion, calling it "a watering down of the women's movement to make it fuckable and palatable for men," as she says in *Diva*. "When I started, people were very defensive, assuming I was a militant, man-hating separatist. It seemed that a woman singing about her own experience was the scariest thing on the planet. Now the music industry has realized that not only do women make music, they buy music. Women are quite a force in the market, and there's a whole commodification of chick singers. . . . So many young women performers out there making a noise don't embrace the term feminist.

Look at them — Jewel, Alanis, PJ Harvey — who knows what the fuck they're thinking? It seems they don't give a shit about how much women had to work before them so they could be there doing what they want to do. It drives me crazy." Despite her caution in using the term feminism, Ani's understanding of the feminist movement is historically informed, as she makes clear in her celebrated article on Joni Mitchell published in the *Los Angeles Times*: "Look at women's lives before the suffragettes got us the right to vote in 1920, and you will see that feminists made things better, not worse. Look at women's lives before the second-wave feminist movement of the 1970s, and you will not see the female politicians, athletes, college students, professionals, musicians, etc., that you do now. This is the living legacy of feminism. It is democracy at work and it is nothing short of inspirational, not unlike Joni Mitchell's life, which has inspired countless young women to artistic honesty and personal and professional strength. . . . One of the great lies of conservatism is that feminism and femininity are somehow in opposition to each other. Feminism is simply the belief that a woman has the right to become herself, just as a man has the right to become himself. All decent people, male and female, are feminists. The only people who are not feminists are those who believe that women are inherently inferior or undeserving of the respect and opportunity afforded me. Either you are a feminist or you are a sexist/misogynist. There is no box marked 'other'."

But the two-edged sword of feminism cuts both ways, even though both blades are a touch dull, as she suggests in *Ms.* magazine: "My idea of feminism is self-determination, and it's very open-ended: every woman has the right to become herself, and do whatever she needs to do. But there are all these righteous babes out there who, if I step in stage in a dress, are infuriated." The overly ardent feminist, the overly possessive lesbian trying to make Ani into her self-image, has been the bane of Ani's outspoken attitude, her willingness to say what's on her mind. So has been the 'red-neck' reaction to her at-times lesbian lifestyle, as she noted in *The Advocate*: "My life was made hell by what I said [about being with women] in those music magazines. Those women's music people did great stuff, but that still didn't make it so I could walk in a bar in Buffalo and start singing about some girl I was in love with and not be called every name in the straight-world book. I still get heat: 'Are you a man hater?'

And it's like, 'OK, let's start at the beginning: Loving a woman doesn't mean hating a man.'" A fine line to walk between possessive (dare we say, obsessive) lesbians and good old dyke-haters.

From the start of her career Ani has been walking this line but never for the sake of doing so, never with the fear of disturbing anyone with her opinions and actions — with her music and lyrics. For Ani, as she's often said in interviews, the question isn't whether she's a lesbian or not. Furthermore, the question should have no relevancy for appreciating her music. And, as a simple listen to her lyrics prove, it doesn't. Like Tom Robinson, another bisexual performer who came under fire when he revealed he didn't strictly follow a predominantly gay lifestyle, the lyrics are left to interpretation. You'll hear a heterosexual woman singing songs of love and loneliness, leaving a dead-beat lover and trying to survive in the face of it all, if that's what you want. As she astutely says in *Monkey Magnet*, "I've always used my music as my sort of litmus test, that if I say this because I am this, then by your reaction I learn so much more about you than if I were to remain appropriate and never say those things." That's the power of great art, to hold up the mirror to us all so we can see ourselves in our reactions.

"I think it is very useful to know ourselves," Ani says in *Rocket Magazine*, "but when we start naming and labeling, that is dangerous, that gets problematic. It negates that things are always changing. Besides, it's hard to pin a label onto something that's always moving." The beauty of Ani's lyrics is their taut introspection. Rarely, do they gravitate specifically on she/she issues. At the core of Ani's experience is her sense of what her own sexuality means to herself. Issues like he/she and she/she don't factor into the equation unless they become a specific part of the lyric. The decision to strictly record a 'lesbian' song isn't deliberate. "I read somewhere that I'm trying to challenge my dyke following by sleeping with a man," Ani says in *The Advocate*. "God, I would never go to such extremes —like there's a straight girl from hell lurking within me. Throughout all this my perception of love has remained consistent: I experience love in a really primal, ungendered way. I've written about it that way, I use both he and she pronouns, I write about people who intrigue and attract me." In the book *Solo*, Ani says, "Lately I've been experiencing this whole new terror because DILATE is mostly about that ridiculous, essential experience of falling in love. The object of my affection happened to be a boy, and that fact gave rise to a whole wave of disillusionment in the dyke community. I had fallen for a guy, so I was suddenly the straight queen of the universe. I heard that a lot of women were getting off the boat because I fell in love with a guy. They saw that as the ultimate betrayal. The really terrifying thing for me was the thought that those women were here all along because, what, I was a sex symbol? That's the thing they got out of what I do? Whoa. I'm still grappling with that thought. It's the ultimate terror to think that there's no difference between me and Mariah Carey other than the people I'm attracting." And as she says in *Hero Magazine*, "Since the beginning of my musical career, I've not really minced words about the areas of my life or the people I've loved or do love. Certainly, it's a big part of it. Whenever a woman sings about loving another woman, there's a whole kind of marginalized desperate group of people, of which I am one, who want to be affirmed in their culture. I know that search myself. So there's a lot of speculation. But it's so funny to me. I've only ever been above board and put my cards on the table, or whatever the cliche is, about who I am." As she says in *Diva*, "I just sing about my life."

Ani DiFranco's choice of music for singing about her life, for speaking out against the world none of us "wants to live in," for "effecting change, providing inspiration, and perpetrating art," has been folk music. How she defines folk music may not be what The Oxford Music Dictionary would have you believe it is, but for her, it's the best tool with which to articulate her viewpoint. In a 1997 *Acoustic Guitar* article, Ani was quoted as saying, "People my age find folk music very uncool. . . . Folk music is not an acoustic guitar — that's not where the heart of it is. I use the word folk in reference to punk music and to rap music. It's an attitude, it's an awareness of one's heritage, and it's a community. It's subcorporate music that gives voice to different communities and their struggle against authority." While being interviewed in *Spin*, Ani commented, "Where I'm from, people are so disgustingly sincere that their music always veers into the corny. The other day, I was trying to think of any folksinger I knew that were assholes and I couldn't think of a single one." But she stops short of becoming a self-righteous folky, laughing at her 'folk' self in a 1994 *Guitar Player* interview: "Having a folk mosh is my favorite thing.

I've actually stage dived at a couple of my shows. The only problem is the music stops!" She does recognize a need to move beyond the stereotype of the L'il Folksinger, standing alone on the stage, as she comments in *Hero Magazine*: "I think my music is starting to journey away from my folk roots in terms of structure and it's becoming more fluid. I think now that I have a killer band and other creative people, I can lay back on the groove a little more and focus on the interaction more, which a solo folk singer doesn't get to do much of." That said, her heroes will always remain Woody Guthrie and Pete Seeger. "I've seen Pete change the world around him," Ani is quoted as saying on the Appleseed Records Homepage. "I've seen him set about fixing things big and small, in an everyday kinda-way. And I think if I've ever known peace in this world, it's been in his voice."

The heart of folk music is language, lyrics, storytelling. Ani's respect for the power of language is profound. In the midst of her essay on Joni Mitchell and feminism published in the *Los Angeles Times*, Ani wrote, "words are some of the most powerful and important things I know. I have spent my life as a songwriter, exercising language. Language is the tool of love and the weapon of hatred. It's the bright red warning flag of danger — and the stone foundation of diplomacy and peace. The manipulation, decoration and revelation of language are what songwriting is all about."

On the power of storytelling, Ani responded enthusiastically during a *Sessions at West 54th* interview: "Yeah. Storytelling. Exactly. I'm really into storytelling. I mean, with a big S, you know, as in oral history. As in parents telling their kids what to do on the planet. I think a lot about storytelling and its value in society, and I see what I do as a little teeny offshoot, or related to that. This is my theory about storytelling. There's stories of the boogie man and the troll under the bridge and great floods and we're all walking around with them now. You know, these are all stories that are passed down from generation to generation. And they tell big truths and little truths. I'm thinking about what I've done and seen and including my little story in this sort of immediate soup of my time and place. I think . . . all of our stories are equally relevant, and the more people there are presenting theirs, the broader our vocabulary, our cultural vocabulary, becomes. I think there's still the folk tradition of keeping history vital through talking about stuff that happened. That's still very alive. But it's not such a big element of pop culture or commercial music."

Folk music has always been politically inspired, politically charged, a direction Ani has been deliberately taking since the release of UPX6. "On this record," she says in a RBR press release interview, "'*Tis Of Thee* and *Come Away From It* play out a dialogue on the drug war, the former from a political perspective and the latter from a personal one. *Come Away For It* was written about my experience of loving and caring for a person who was hellbent on self-annihilation. The two songs are in no way contradictory, they are simply two varied perspectives on the same theme. Anyone who has intimate experience with drug addiction knows that fighting it is not a right wing-left wing thing, it's a self-preservation thing. Anyway, drugs are not inherently the problem; drug overuse is more a symptom of looming psychological, personal, economic, or societal problems than it is the cause. The government's ' throw them all in jail and make the problem disappear' policy is not making our streets safer or helping out people. We have to help ourselves and each other to not fall prey to drug addiction even when it seems like the most logical and informed way of dealing with our ugly little lives." Ani's recent lyrics have taken on the hue of traditional folk song subjects and themes, often mentioning the role of the little guys, those at the bottom of the socio-economical level. Her work with Utah Phillips on FELLOW WORKERS gave Ani a glimpse into the past of an America very few people really know. In a RBR press release interview for FELLOW WORKERS, she says, "As the album was making itself around us, it seemed to be developing a focus of 20th century American labor history, and as we move into the 21st century I hope that the true history of working people will not be forgotten. After all, we need these old stories of solidarity, struggle and victory to instruct and inspire us in our consciousness even today. The way I figure it, 'the boss' may have mutated from a cigar-chomping, suspender-snapping mogul into a nameless, faceless (hard to point at and hold accountable) multinational corporation. But little about the power dynamic therein has changed. The Exxons and McDonaldses are no more concerned with, or responsible to, us, our communities and our environment, than the Rockefellers were to the miners and their families in the decimating coal mines of West Virginia in the 1930s. This being said, I think that Mother Jones, armed with her mops and brooms, has something to teach us, even now, about our own liberty and humanity in the face of exploitive, dehumanizing economic powers."

Ani's late 1999 album release, TO THE TEETH, addresses poignant themes at the heart of today's headlines. *Hello Birmingham*, a song Ani premiered on the F-Word Tour, deals with abortion, not as a personal event as in *Lost Woman Song* from her first album, but as a political one, as she explains in the February 1999 issue of *CMJ*. "The big picture is getting alarmingly big for me. It's very humbling for me to not necessarily feel like you have the space to be right about anything. This recent shooting in Buffalo, the abortion doctor (Arnold Slepian), I think in times past I would've been up on rooftops screaming about what was going on. And I've noticed that my reaction to this now is, 'Okay, it's just become too dangerous.' Women in this city are not safe. Women in Birmingham, Alabama, are not safe. Women across the border in Hamilton, Ontario, are not safe. I think that people who believe in women's freedom of choice need to go on a really concerted effort to reach out. There's so much divisiveness, so much non-listening that goes on. I think our new strategy has got to be, 'We respect your morality, we respect your opinions. To be against abortion is totally fine; we understand that, we sympathize with that. We just think everyone needs to make that decision for themselves.' No one of us can tell all of us how to be or what to think. We cannot dictate each other's morality. I feel more mortally scared and sad about the recent events because I think the battle has got to end."

But Ani DiFranco knows the battle will go on. She will continue to find inspiration from the way the righteous work to change this world into a place where we all want to live. "I always was an activist," she says in *Ms.* magazine, "and whenever I get bogged down, I look at all those progressive lawyers I know who work in death-penalty resource centers, or my friends who work at rape crisis centers or hospitals and AIDS wards. There are so many people doing work like that who don't get applause at the end of the day. Those are the people I draw my inspiration from."

SUPERHERO

"When I started writing my songs," Ani once told *Girlfriends* magazine, "the people who responded to me first and the strongest were my tribe of younger women. I got all hooked in, year after year, in this community. But then I noticed that after a while, my job had become to stand on stage and have a sea of bald-headed overall-wearing baby dykes screaming at me. I could predict exactly which lines would get a response and only one side of my songs was being affirmed. I was starting to feel like a cartoon. Not like I'm trying to characterize all my audience like that. Please let it be known that I love them. I love my fans. All I have to do is go to other peoples' shows to realize how lucky I am to have my fans, how much energy they give me back. But the front five rows contain a lot of over-bearing enthusiastic women who are responding to one side of me and then other parts of me cease to exist. It makes me feel lonely and disrespected. The cheering section was trying to reduce me to being a symbol of one thing rather than a human struggling with many things. So I started going in another direction. My life has changed a lot. I stopped hanging out with a lot of young women other than my oldest friends. And I'm totally madly in love with my partner. I call my last tour my 'shut up and calm down tour'. I swear I had to say that more than once. Several nights there were women right in front who kept screaming at me, throwing things at me. One night in particular I couldn't take it anymore and I knelt down and said to one of these women, 'please give me a break. I'm trying to do my job and you're making it really hard for me." And I felt terrible because I knew her heart sank and I was devastated to be pushed that far. She disappeared for a while but by the end of the show she was up front again and I knelt down to her again and said, 'hey, no hard feelings, okay?' And she said, 'I understand. It's okay.' When I get onstage I get truth tourrettes. I just start saying whatever I'm thinking. It gets me in some sticky situations sometimes; I mean, I understand where my fans are coming from. I realize how important it is to have yourself affirmed whether through books or music or whatever. So I understand their reaction. But at the same time, it's a Catch 22 for me. It's an interesting struggle, an ongoing dialogue."

Ani DiFranco's relationship with her fans is indeed complex. While she inspires idolatry unwittingly from one group, she aspires for respect from another. Her typical fan is female, aged between fifteen and thirty, well-educated (or plans on being very well-educated). The age demarcations aren't universals, they're just variables that help to narrow our observations. Her fans (and, to some degree, everybody else's I suppose) can be divided into two camps: the Devout Worshippers and (to borrow a phrase from Wiccan philosophy) the Solitary Practitioner.

Devout Worshippers praise the Goddess at the Altar. Ani is their Patron Saint of Understanding. They worship the Diva (as she's so often called on fan web sites) and gravitate on her every word, hinge on her every performance, live-eat-sleep-breathe Ani stuff all the time. They believe in her over and above and beyond the call of the everyday. They've been referred to as the "Ani police" by one fan on the DiFranco Message Board on the Internet. These are the fans who openly reviled Alana Davis when she released her own, slightly rewritten version of *32 Flavors*. Surf the web and look through any given fan's homepage, and almost always, there's the picture of Alana Davis with a circle/red line through it. The Ani police were unforgiving in their hatred. The song was a vile thing, how dare she rewrite it (Ani approved the rewrite), etc. etc. When an MTV film crew showed up at an Ani concert, an angered fan shouted out, "What are THEY doing here?" There's genuine fear in place: they don't want Ani taken away.

Some fans indeed fear Ani has been kidnapped by corporate forces. They fear being betrayed by her. Her fans responded passionately and negatively towards the presence of her standard *Amazing Grace* on a CD sold to patrons of The Gap in 1996 when they learned of the existence of the disc when an eBay auction site offered it up for sale over the Internet. Instantly, her fan base split into two distinct factions: those who gave a rat's ass and those who didn't. Unforgiving fans were quick to admonish Ani for the move, calling it the worst kind of sell-out imaginable. A large portion of her fan base likes to consider itself anti-establishment. And for them, The Gap, one of the free world's biggest clothing chains, epitomizes a uniform world where everyone wears cookie-cutter outfits as determined by the manufacturer. Other fans, offering up a far more world-weary explanation, admitted they found nothing wrong with the move and were quick to realize that the GAP CD was a savvy promotion device, not evidence of Ani being compromised by The Man.

A second fan crisis of this nature related to the use of *32 Flavors* (Ani's version of her own song) for the NFL promo TV spots which aired in December 1998. RBR had authorized the NFL's use of the song in their spots, thinking the request to be "funny" and a "different" way for them (RBR) to promote Ani's music. Again, many fans weren't so amused. Some used the words "sell-out" again. So much so, rumor had it, that RBR were in re-think mode and unsure as to whether licensing of this sort would ever occur in the future.

Because Ani's music deals with personal emotions, there exists a degree of identification in each and every song. That doesn't mean that anyone who's ever had an abortion can relate to *Lost Woman Song* better than someone who hasn't. But the level of intensity with regards to how we view a song is directly proportional to our own given life experiences. Think of any artist you know who has painted an image you like. That image speaks to you in varying degrees. If you love it, you experience an intense identification with the singer.

Most of these fans are also very intolerant of artists they see as potential threats to the L'il Folksinger's career. There's an even split as to who is more hated, Alanis Morissette, Jewel Kilcher, or Tori Amos. And while that may not seem like such a big deal (or not have any impact on Ani's music itself), it does cause a certain amount of diversion to occur. At the core of the hatred stems the life experiences of these performers: Morissette's "spoiled little rich kid who started on Canadian TV" past, Jewel's "cutesy-pie" look, Amos' surrealism. Let's not paint something more than what it is: the rantings of passionate individuals who fail to take into account a broader picture. Devout Worshippers have it in for anyone who would tamper/damage/endanger Ani's world and Ani herself. Cruise through the message boards on anidifranco.net and you read the musings, ramblings and free-form thoughts of a whole community of Anifans in effervescent thought and raw emotional upheaval. Boyfriend/girlfriend issues predominate, with fans asking how they should treat lovers, both unrequited and mutual. Some fans bemoan the home front and how they've failed to communicate with either parent. Ani's lyrics appear in support, bold companions on introspective journeys. For many DWs, the lyrics are like epithets of wisdom, words handed down from on high, like commandments issued to Moses from Mount Sinai. DWs find solace in their candor, humor in their scathing wit and Ani's infectious laughter, succour for their soul's ailments.

Janine (real names of fans as follows have been changed to protect myself, my publisher, and the individual) is a devout Ani fan. She's down-loaded the guitar tabs off the Internet and wants to be just like Ani. Janine is fourteen. To her, Ani is The Diva. She's that lone voice of reason, understanding, non-judgment in a sea of confusion, despair, and contra-dictory emotions. At fourteen, Janine hasn't many friends. She thinks adults in her life don't have the time or patience to sit down and talk to her. She tried leaving home once before but was caught just as she was exiting the back door. I asked her what it was about Ani that she liked.

"Ani is so much better than anybody else on the scene right now," she e-mailed me. "Ani is a superb guitarist, an amazing singer and this totally cool person. She doesn't take no shit from anybody. She's not into image or style. She don't care if she's happening or not. She's not like, duh, The Spice Girls. You know, that crazy, fake 'girl power' stuff."

I had asked her how many of Ani's albums she had. "All of them. I started by buying LITTLE PLASTIC CASTLE because somebody played that song on the high school radio station. I found out who it was and went to the mall to get it right away. I'm from a small town in Alberta. It was easy to find LITTLE PLASTIC CASTLE. But the other albums were a little harder to find. I had to travel to Edmonton, and then the store I usually go when I'm there had to order them. I really got into IMPERFECTLY. So much of what she wrote there touched me in a unique way. It's like she knows what I'm thinking."

"Do you listen to any other artists in the same category?"

"I bought Beth Orton's CENTRAL RESERVATION last month cause a friend of mine told me it was like really hot right now. It was alright, but it didn't kick butt the way *Shy* does. I don't think anybody else can capture that introspective thing as well as she can."

A later phone conversation (she reached me via e-mail and asked me if she could talk to me over the phone) led to more questions. Janine doesn't much care for the Utah Phillips albums. "They were okay. But I guess I expected more. I don't listen to them all that often. She plays some nice licks on some of the songs." What about the whole Alana Davis *32 Flavors* issue? "Ugh, let's *not* go there and say we did," she stated matter-of-factly.

Does she hope to one day have the kind of career Ani does?

"Wouldn't that be, like, the ultimate?"

Janine is a sharp, intelligent teen, a mind in total effervescence that yearns for wider pastures. Her "la-di-da" parents (her words, not mine) stay out of her way with stilted indifference. She does okay at school but wants to go the music route.

"You realize very few people make it as big as, say, Madonna. Is that what you want to achieve?" I asked her.

"Oh," she brushes the question off, "I know that. I don't care."

Brendan (name changed upon request), is, admittedly, homosexual. To him, Ani's music was a badge of honor and an affirmation that no matter what sexual orientation you are, you can achieve a certain degree of success with dignity and vision. He first heard of Ani through a lesbian friend and started to attend the shows whenever she came to town. Many of his male friends aren't really into the so-called "gay" or "lesbian" music scenes.

"It's not like me and my boyfriends sat around listening to Donna Summer or Tom Robinson all day. You know . . . the myth that all gay guys listen to Broadway show tunes. That's such a load of shit."

But Ani's marriage to Andy Gilchrist left Brendan slightly confused over what the singer's true intentions were. He felt betrayed somewhat.

"I know she didn't do it on purpose. But it kinda leaves a sour taste in the mouth, y'know?" he admitted to me while we shared cappuccinos at one of the book store/coffee houses in Richmond Hill. "I know it kinda happens, I mean, love is never as predictable as one thinks and all that. But some of my friends really questioned her motives for writing the songs."

Today, Brendan doesn't listen to her music much. "I lost interest when she tried to funk things up. She just stopped being relevant, original or interesting. I mean, at the core of what she sings about is still this ' I-love-you-but-I-hate-you' ambivalence. And now she's happily married. . . . Makes one wonder."

I described my view of what I thought Ani-fans were all about and he agreed to some degree. "I guess I was a Devout Worshipper," he admitted. "For the longest time I thought she was the only artist who was able to actually write a decent song. Especially during the grunge scene. I was only eighteen when she released DILATE and I had already come out of the closet. For me, the albums just prior to DILATE were her most vibrant ones, the ones that I thought were filled with insight and meaning. I still own those albums on compact disc. I just treat them the way I do my Smiths albums . . . I just don't listen to them all that much. I went on with my life."

Solitary Practitioners may also worship Ani, but it's the worship of respect and maturity. Ani helped them get through the crises of high school, their own sexuality, whatever. They love her songs for their candor, their literacy, their universality. But they hardly think that Ani is the only one capable of such forthrightness. They glean more from Ani's DIY creativity and use that independence to anchor their own lives. They don't worship the Diva at the altar. They respect everything she's worked for, everything she's fought for, everything she stands for. But they aren't as reverential as the Devout Worshipper. A fan admitted that it was probably cruel to post "See Ani Nude" tags on his web site. He was just curious to see how many hits he'd get (473). And when the SP fan gets upset, he/she just goes away from the net community. "The message board has become very evil so it has now been closed," wrote a disgruntled fan. "If people had been nicer and more civilized it would have stayed up, in fact the entire site may go down if things continue this way. I remember when being an Ani fan was fun and her music had meaning, now it is all full of people showing their hatred for one another. . . . This was a nice little place I set up with my own funds and time for all of you to enjoy, but you abused it and you abused me, so I no longer want to run it." Someone else started up the Message Board and it is filled with rampant idiocy by very small-minded people (and by other fans who are sincere in their views). It's that small-mindedness that makes the Solitary Practitioner crazy. There is a righteous tone in their voices. But it isn't about how Ani is Goddess Incarnate. It's about the things that make our world a better place. It's something as simple as posting information on the proper etiquette at an upcoming Ani concert. On the anidifranco.net message board, these people respond with kindness, understanding, and worthwhile information.

Sarah got into Ani DiFranco thanks to a friend who loaned her a copy of DILATE. At nineteen, Sarah wants, like Janine, to become a successful singer-songwriter. Ani's DIY ethic and her strong personality make Ani a worthy model for Sarah. While Sarah listens to many other artists, she currently feels Ani is her favorite. She likes the lyrics the most.

"I find them so easy to relate to," she told me during a phone conversation. "They hit me in all the right emotional places. Especially *Not A Pretty Girl*. I just find she has a very level head on her shoulders. Everything she writes is so personal and direct. I don't know . . . I just feel deeply moved by what she sings about."

Sarah saw Ani in concert for the first time during Ani's Toronto stop on the F-Word tour with Maceo Parker. "What an incredible show," she proclaimed. "I went all by myself and I thought I would be a little nervous about it. But it turned out to be really personal and special."

"Were there many teens?"

"More like, people in their thirties and forties. I know that sounds weird, but I saw more older people than I did teenagers. There was this really great atmosphere. It definitely had a sing-a-long like quality about it."

Ask her about the Alana Davis situation and she admits to being bugged by Davis' version of the song. "But I think too many people made a big deal out of it. I mean, I heard Davis' version of the song before I'd even heard Ani DiFranco. I liked it. But when I heard Ani's version, it was hard to go back and hear Davis' take on it."

As for Ani's sexuality, Sarah admits she could care less. "Besides," she said, "I don't think it has very much to do with what she sings about."

Then there's Chloe, an Anifan of another kind and one of my wife's clients. When Lynda told her I was writing a book about Ani, the short hairs at the back of Chloe's neck bristled.

"I liked Ani, once," she began. Lynda asked Chloe to write down the rest. Literate and impassioned, her letter is reproduced in full here because of Chloe's intense feelings for Ani and how Ani has affected her day-to-day life as a lesbian. Once seen by Chloe as the champion of her lifestyle, Ani has betrayed her and herself, as Chloe sees things. Her passionate attachment to Ani is not atypical, nor is her sense of betrayal, among Ani's lesbian fans.

I used to love Ani DiFranco. She spoke to me and I could relate to her music and to her world. Not anymore.

I'm 30, and I am a lesbian. I'm comfortable with this; it is my true self, no lies, no indecision. When I first heard Ani, I was enlivened and encouraged. She seemed to be so sure of herself and of her world. And of her sexuality. Now I believe that it was all fabricated, that she used the lesbian "angle" to sell records, be controversial and to "appeal" to a crowd of people, namely lesbians, who could validate her in some way. I take offence to her being on an album called WOMEN LIKE US, which celebrates singers who write about the lesbian experience, when she is openly *not* a lesbian and is now married. How can you say you're one thing and then be another? Everything she seems to do is filled with contradictions. I understand that people grow and change, but I feel cheated. She is not the same person she used to be, fundamentally. It used to be about the "little people" out there. Not anymore. She doesn't *need* to sell out to a major record company. She's creating one all by herself. I mean, if she's really just a "little folk singer," then why is one of her songs on a big movie soundtrack?

I don't know why, but with the album DILATE, things changed. She changed. And she never explained why she changed to us "little people" whom she claims really matter. Or did I miss something?

It's not that I don't wish her well or that I don't wish her fame and fortune. But I don't understand why she felt she had to jettison her "lesbianism" in order to achieve it.

I read in the press that she was upset that "we lesbians" felt this way about her now. I wonder if she knew how I felt when she told the world that her sexuality was a "whatever" thing. It never was a "whatever" thing for me and my lover. It's bad enough that we have to strive to find our own voices for ourselves. But to have people like Ani DiFranco come along and throw in a lot of ambiguity regarding what we're all about just demeans us further in the eyes of people who don't understand us.

— *Chloe*

Jason is a forty-three-year-old man who loves folk music. He's seen Ani a handful of times, in small settings and larger venues. He owns almost all of her recordings. He paints in his spare time and writes poetry.

"Not anywhere as perfect as Ani's I'm afraid," he told me in a phone conversation we had back at the start of the summer of 1999.

"Have you thought about writing music, or singing or . . . ?"

"Not in the least. I've got no voice whatsoever."

What are his thoughts about the "in or out" nature of Ani's sexuality? "I never really gave it much thought. I mean, rock artists like David Bowie or Elton John or Mick Jagger have had loads of controversy over their sexual escapades. Does Elton John being a homosexual make *Bennie And The Jets* or *Tiny Dancer* less great? I don't think so. I don't really hear the words in a he/she or he/he or she/she sort of context. I hear them for what they are, I think. They're the words of a soul in free-thought."

He found out about Ani when he read an article on her which was published by *Dirty Linen*, the folk music magazine. "She sounded genuine. That's a rare commodity in musicians these days."

Immediately, Jason was struck with they way Ani sang and the intensity of the songs. It crossed the same terrain as singers he'd admired his whole life. "You know, people like Eric Andersen, The Band, James Taylor. She'd probably hate to think she was on the same level as James Taylor, but the way I hear a song like *Shy* is the way I hear James Taylor sing *Something In The Way She Moves* or Eric Andersen singing *Thirsty Boots*. It was cool to see her on the same stage as Bob Dylan. It kind of felt good to see two generations traversing the same terrain." For Jason, Ani is the new voice in this folk tradition. Ani's words are as intense as Joni Mitchell's, as passionate as Dylan's, as political as Woody Guthrie's. She's the next evolutionary step in a progression that has weathered the rise and fall of punk, new wave, new country, and grunge.

From her words, actions, and recordings, Ani DiFranco appears to be a woman in a state of perpetual quest. Trying to find the joy, happiness, and fulfilment of a life lived well, with honor and decency, lived in total abandonment to the "me" of being. This quest is not the narcissistic mumblings of a spoiled brat who's just mirroring the sentiments of her generation. This is the soul of that generation as typified by one individual's power and vision in the face of adversity. If there's anything positive to be said of Gen-X'ers as they hit their early thirties, it is that they possess the imaginative tools to deconstruct the world the Baby Boomers built.

My many conversations with Anifans in their twenties, as well as many of my peers in that age group, leave me somewhat confident about the future of music and of thought in general. It's a generation used to seeing it all played out in front of them on television and in the movies. They don't accept the bullshit trappings of a culture now into Tae Bo or power veggie meals. They listen to music in a disposable fashion, *except* for their heroes. Then, they become passionate and intelligent. But not brainwashed. They've learned to shrug off the mass media bombardment. Boomers call it a "slacker" mentality. In reality, it's the defense mechanism of a generation trying to find its own voice, the way Boomers did with their own parents a generation earlier. Ani DiFranco, in that sense, is very much a product of her generation. She takes no shit from those levels of the world which would abuse her, use her, control her, subjugate her. Often, time and again, I hear this from twentysomethings. Many feel that Boomers are nothing more than money-grubbing consumers with very little tolerance for a broader culture. If twentysomethings embrace gangsta rap as easily as reggae or Ricky Martin-type Latino-discofunk, or the musings of a passionate, 'discourseful' woman like Ani DiFranco, it's because it is the antithesis of what their parents would do. Their Boomer parents would have no truck with Ani's tattoos, pierced nose, bisexual past, or DIY ethic. In the final analysis, Ani is her own boss, sings in her own voice, designs and shapes the world around her in her own fashion, as each and every one of us does. That she's achieved success isn't that unusual. That she still keeps her sense of righteousness with her is.

"I feel less and less righteous about everything," Ani says in a February 1999 interview in *CMJ*, "which is not to say I feel any less dedicated to political change. I find it hard. It's scary to think . . . as people get older they get less angry and they're just like fuckin' triple A radio." Recognizing this danger, there is little chance Ani will abandon her beliefs, her seemingly innate sense of righteousness. Righteousness is defined by the clarity of the individual's vision of what is just and decent. Righteousness means empowerment, determination, fighting the good fight, a voice howling against the ramparts articulating the screams of the silent majority. The voice The Weavers sang in. Joan Baez sang in. Bob Dylan sang in. Joni Mitchell sang in. Kurt Cobain sang in. The voice of the soul.

THE LI'L OLD ANI DIFRANCO PRESSKIT
winter 1999

from the depth of the pacific to the height of everest...

Ani's art, opinions, and image have been featured
in a wide variety of publications, as shown in this
Righteous Babe Records press kit and elsewhere.

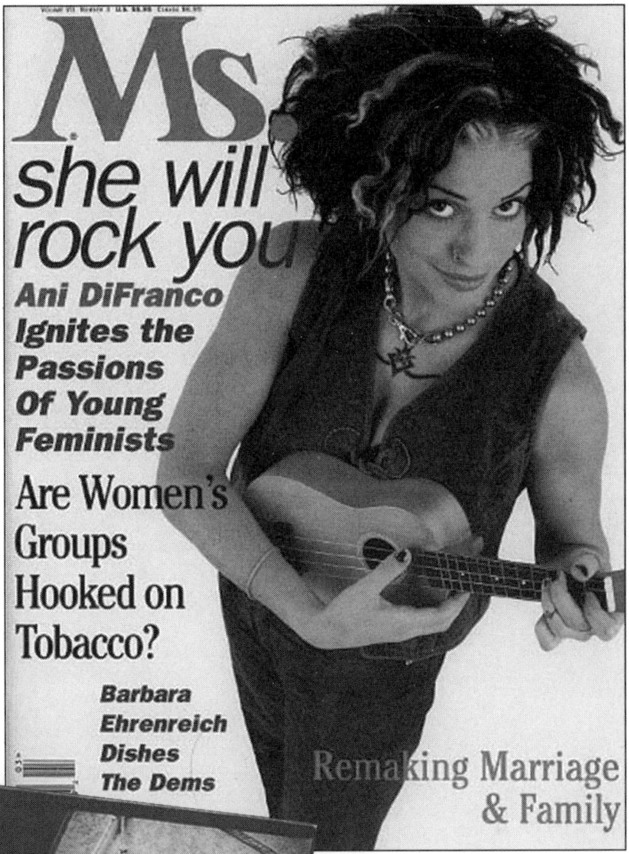

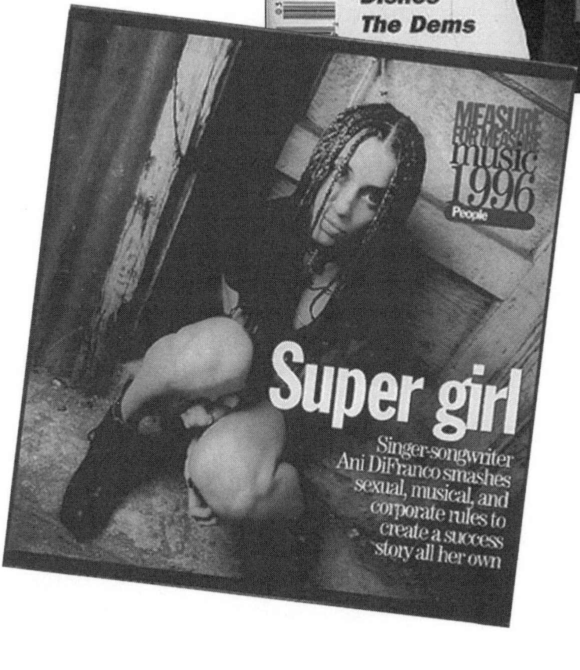

Images of Ani, from Spin, Solo, Ms, *and* People.

ani difranco

UP
UP
UP
UP

the new album
on righteous babe records

Living In Sound Clip

i speak without reservation from what i know and who i am. i do so with the understanding that all people should have the right to offer their voice to the chorus whether the result is harmony or dissonance. the worldsong is a colorless dirge without the differences which distinguish us, and it is that difference which should be celebrated not condemned. should any part of my music offend you, please do not close your ears to it. just take what you can and go on.

— Ani DiFranco, from ANI DIFRANCO

A critical review of Ani DiFranco's recording career, album by album, song by song, shows she has never deviated from the statement of purpose she proclaimed on the sleeve of her first self-titled CD. Almost ten years and more than ten albums later Ani still speaks without reservation, though her music has undergone considerable change, evolving from the lone guitar and voice of the folksinger to the driving power of a band. While the music may have changed somewhat, she remains a poet whose lyrics provoke response and invite interpretation. Tracing the thematic motifs and the play of language in her 'collected' works shows that she ranks among the greatest of folksingers, taking her place beside Joni Mitchell, her idol, or Utah Phillips, her collaborator, or even Bob Dylan, her tour side-kick, in the folk-rock-pop pantheon. Or taking her place in the company of contemporary women singer-songwriters, like Alanis Morissette, Tori Amos, Sarah McLachlan, Lucinda Williams, and the others who give context to Ani's achievement, those who may have influenced her, those she may be influencing today. This review of her musical and lyrical achievement includes a discussion of this context.

All of Ani's albums are available from her own record company: Righteous Babe Records. While cassette and (in a few limited titles) vinyl versions of her albums are available (also via Righteous Babe), this critical review of her recorded works covers only those titles currently on compact disc. Album titles and catalog numbers are based on North American activity only, though Ani's albums are available in most of the civilized world in reasonably well-stocked record stores. Album titles are followed by the year of release and catalog number. Further information on the availability of any of Ani's releases can be obtained by contacting Righteous Babe Records at P.O. Box 95, Ellicott Station, Buffalo NY, 14205, USA, or by dialing 1-800-ON-HER-OWN.

SHE'S TRYING TO SING JUST ENOUGH

ANI DIFRANCO
(RBR001-D) 1990 (CD 1992)

Both Hands (3:38)	Rush Hour (5:03)
Talk To Me Now (4:29)	Fire Door (2:42)
The Slant (1:36)	The Story (3:30)
Work Your Way Out (4:08)	Every Angle (2:44)
Dog Coffee (2:56)	Out of Habit (2:45)
Lost Woman Song (4:50)	Letting The Phone Ring (4:30)
Pale Purple (4:02)	(CD bonus song)

For her first album, originally released on cassette in 1990, Ani chose to go it alone with only her voice and her guitar work. Dale Anderson's production keeps it tight with just Ani, a microphone and her guitar. The twelve songs (*Letting The Phone Ring* was added as a bonus cut on the CD reissue) benefitted from superb recording thanks to up-close miking and a solid sense of space. The CD graphic shows a photo of Ani in full contemplation, a bare hint of her infamous smile present. The eyes look wary, unsure while her name appears in scribbled capital letters. And while some may consider these numbers the work of a "naive" artist, there isn't a single moment where one feels in the presence of something other than a sure artist in full control of voice and song.

The strong, visual images, accentuated by percussive stabs of notes strummed hard on the guitar, were to set the tone for subsequent albums (until she started hiring backup musicians). Eventually, this style would form the basis for Ani's folk-punk *sturm und drang*. On her first album, Ani showed she wasn't afraid of mincing words, of painting landscapes of fear, dread, loathing, disgust, and ambivalence while seeking the truth (especially to one's self) and a nobility in life despite all the odds. Of being "on her own" in a world not of her choosing. This sense of alienation would resurface often on subsequent releases.

Drawn from an immense wellspring of personal experiences, the first album is a classic of modern folk, on par with impressive debuts from Suzanne Vega, The Indigo Girls, and Beth Orton.

Both Hands, the lead off track, stands as the account of two lovers who fail to communicate despite the world listening in on their conversations and amorous activities, namely the "old woman" listening in on the airshaft from the first floor. Bold strums of the guitar accentuate Ani's poetic lyrics: "your bones have been my bed frame / and your flesh has been my pillow."

Talk To Me Now uses the first person and stands as testimony to Ani's first adventures in New York (where she doesn't avert her eyes to anyone or hike up her skirt). Much of the wordplay stems from Ani's fear of losing her own identity in the face of a world not of her choosing (and where she was born a woman): "in this city / self preservation / is a full-time occupation."

The Slant is an audio-poem without musical accompaniment. "i am a work in progress," she states in word-play that mixes the fantastic with the everyday.

Work Your Way Out, a moody ballad sung in hushed tones and muted whispers, stands as a song about not needing advice from anyone. "you just start on the inside / and work your way out," Ani advises.

Dog Coffee, the first of many Ani diatribes against government control, portrays a woman "perpetrating counter-culture" and "pushing poems at the urban silence," challenging the face of authority, "the word from washington every day." Again, curt strummings accent staccato-syllabled words about how people are expendable. The day-to-day existence is the "dog coffee" where some of the beans are "off," showing that even a mundane existence isn't without its perils.

Lost Woman Song, subtitled "For Lucille Clifton," is a story-song about a young woman closing her bank account to pay for an abortion at a clinic. The narrator talks about passing through picketers, "just another woman lost" who's trying to reclaim some of the power she has abandoned. "i am here to exercise my freedom of choice," Ani sings as if she needed to say the words aloud to ensure their potency. She laments the presence of her male partner and loathes the touch of the man's shoulder against her own, but consoles herself in saying "some of life's best lessons / are learned at the worst times." Then Ani meets Lucille Clifton, a clinic worker, finding in her a sympathetic, non-judgmental soul. The clinic's since been closed, laments the narrator. "i don't think that there's one of them / who leads a life that's free of mistakes," Ani sings about the picketers. Her voice then soars over slowly winding guitar notes. More than any other song Ani has written, this one stands as the testimony of a soul in conflict. To those who know that Ani weathered the storm of actually crossing a line of anti-abortion (or Pro-Life) protesters, the song achieves both a sad and sorrowful stance. It is the song of a tortured soul fighting to keep her body and her very being to herself, away from those who would deny her pain, her sorrow, her grief. That the narrator finds succor in the comforting touch of Lucille Clifton shows that there are still some souls who avoid pre-judging, choosing instead to be a compassionate voice among the shouts of anger outside.

Any song following *Lost Woman Song* would stand to lose something, but *Pale Purple* takes the turmoil of her own teen pregnancy back on to the street, into the heart of America: "she says everything is grey here / and nothing is green / the girls down the street / fifteen, seventeen years old / you can smell them getting pregnant / you can hear their rock and roll / that's america." It's a stunning image of our society, but despite this "grey" view, the singer still looks for hope: "but i'm looking for green / just like every human being." Ani's experience growing up in Buffalo and moving to New York ("alone in the city . . . immune to new friendships") has certainly made her wary of the world, to say the least. Innocence was lost long ago.

Rush Hour seems, at first listen, to be a simple, sad love ballad. But dig beneath the words and powerful images appear, images of complacency (the rush hour traffic and the chiming of alarm bells), of love lost and withered (she longs for her boyfriend's leather boots to beat the platform of the downtown train station), of wishing for more from life (a tryst with a woman results in a one night stand that means far more to the narrator than her lover). The real theme here isn't the "shocking" ambivalence of a lesbian relationship within the confines of a heterosexual one. The real theme is the odd compulsion to hide one's true feelings: "there were some things that i / did not tell him / there were certain things he did not / need to know." The song seems to be almost overloaded with ambivalent feelings and disparate images, ending with one of Ani's more perplexing word plays: "make me laugh, make me cry, enrage me / but just don't try to disengage me."

Again, with *Fire Door*, Ani's staccato guitar notes underscore the contemplations of someone feeling lonely: "i am singing now / because my tear ducts are too tired." Post relationship blues. The narrator begs for someone to know how she feels, knowing she's just another statistic in the game of love: "i make such a good statistic / someone should study me now."

Confronted with the usual pick up lines and the usual stares, a woman turns away from talking to someone she's just met in the song *The Story*, admonishing him: "this street is not a market / and i am not a commodity." Besides this strong feminist message, the song reflects upon Ani's process of writing songs: "i am sounding out the silence / avoiding all the words / i'm afraid i can never say enough / i'm afraid no one has heard me."

Every Angle, an uncharacteristically upbeat ballad, sees the singer (a woman) longing for the touch, sight, and smell of her man. "somebody tell this photograph of you / to let go of my eyes," Ani sings, doing a complete 180 spin on the usual "I'm pining for you while I'm looking at your picture" image so prevalent in modern pop love songs.

On *Out Of Habit*, the singer quietly sips a cup of so-called coffee at a bar, while a man notices her hands and asks if she can play (one assumes he also sees the guitar). The singer says okay, but cautions him in quick wordplay, "i said if you don't come any closer / i don't mind if you stay / my thighs have been involved / in many accidents / and now i can't get insured / and I don't need to be lured by you / my cunt is built / like a wound that won't heal." Set in the context of *Lost Woman Song* and *Pale Purple*, these lines resonate with pain. "I don't want to sing for you any more," she laments. The poem ends bitterly: "fuck this time and place / the butter melts out of habit / the toast isn't even warm."

"you are capable of things i could not do", the singer admonishes her boyfriend in *Letting The Telephone Ring*, the CD's closing bonus track. "how could i be so naive," Ani sings in this story of love lost, for "wondering what was wrong / what was wrong." Once her source of inspiration ("i have written so much about you . . . words like water used to flow"), he now leaves her feeling betrayed ("now vicariously i have her in me / i want to peel off my skin / let the water wash in"). Ani would explore this feeling of profound disappointment in love on her next album, NOT SO SOFT.

NOT SO SOFT
(RBR002-D) 1991

Anticipate (3:20)	Roll With It (3:47)
Rockabye (4:32)	Itch (3:01)
She Says (3:36)	Gratitude (3:13)
Make Me Stay (3:10)	The Whole Night (2:47)
On Every Corner (4:19)	The Next Big Thing (3:40)
Small World (3:33)	Brief Bus Stop (3:40) (CD bonus song)
Not So Soft (2:00)	Looking For The Holes (3:32)

For the follow-up to ANI DIFRANCO, the L'il Folksinger returned to Audio Magic Studio in Buffalo during the course of September 1991 and recorded thirteen tracks (a fourteenth bonus track, *Brief Bus Stop*, was added to the CD release). If the title seemed a representation of a change in direction, then the songs live up to expectations. There is no sophomore slump as Ani sings, plays guitar, hits congas, and performs on "dust broom." Dale Anderson returned as producer (Ani takes a co-credit), while Tony Romano handled engineering duties. Ani designed the artwork, while photos from Scot Fisher and Karen Richardson graced the graphics. If the cover graphics seemed slightly spartan, the scribbled capital letters continue to say to the world, "I'm doing it all by myself!" But at the heart of Ani's cover art is someone who knows the mannerisms of drawing and the intricacies and nuances of shading. The double tracking of Ani's voice sets up a warmer feel and actually underscores many of the woman-to-woman love songs contained on this follow-up.

Anticipate takes up right where the first album left off. Again, just Ani and her guitar. The song is yet another of her infamous "be wary of everyone you trust" numbers. "we lose sight of everything / when we have to keep / checking our backs," Ani laments, but holds on to hope: "i think we should just smile / come clean and relax."

Rockabye, a slow-fast tune with interesting chord changes, stands as another looking-through-my-window songs. Here, Ani double-tracks her voice and creates a work of simple yet effective beauty, a personal lullaby: "rockabye, rockabye baby / rockabye the baby that is me / rockabye, rockabye baby / rockabye until i'm fast asleep." Ani's eyes are a camera to the world beneath her window. Her soul is aflutter with ambivalence as she remembers someone who was just with her moments before. The rain, the dark, South Brooklyn day-to-day life. It's like a still-life painting or one of those camera verité images.

She Says is a poignant story of two women who have just enjoyed a passionate moment: one wants the other to stay, the other realizes the moment cannot last. "you know I have no vacancy / and it's awfully cold outside tonight," she says, a stark counterpoint to the lovemaking that went on before. Ani's voice here is that of a wanderer, a woman who cannot commit to more than a mere moment of happiness. Underlying it is the broodiness of the singer, the way the singer doesn't want anything deeper and more intense. "maybe someday, maybe somehow," the narrator sings at the close of the song, but you suspect that moment, that someday, will never come.

Make Me Stay presents the image of a woman who is in the process of leaving her companion, another moment in the course of a love affair, like a VCR on pause. The singer waits for the other to talk her out of going, knowing that this is what is expected: "yes, i'm going to turn / and walk away / you can watch me go / or make me stay." The power of these love songs, and this one in particular, is the intense sense of sadness following lovemaking. This song shows us two people in trouble: the singer because of her "should I stay or should I go? It's all up to you" attitude, and the subject of the song, whose predictable behavior smacks of desperation and loneliness. These are not good feelings to have in order for love to survive. And, in Ani's skilled voice, she neither condemns the other for her predictability, nor herself for her ambivalence.

On Every Corner comes on strong thanks to Ani's soapbox delivery. It's a traditional folk song dressed up in '90s imagery: HIV and AIDS, drug abuse and teen pregnancy. It's the first time in any of her early songs that she waxes philosophical (the anti-choice picketers of Lost Woman Song don't count). "how will they define / our generation / in the coming decades," Ani asks, "who will tell the story." No doubt, she has appointed herself to this role. Later, Ani sings, "our actions will define us / before a single definition / can be said."

On Small World, two women (friends) share remembrances of things past as they talk at the curb of a street they know all too well but for different reasons. At the core of the song lies, in the way these two women remain friends, a kernel of truth Ani delivers in the last two lines: "i said sister looks to me / like you're going to be fine." The listener doesn't expect that level of sympathy and encouragement, turning the tough things these two women have been through into something inconsequential.

The title track, Not So Soft, comes on at first like another of Ani's infamous rants. The city is a corporate jungle, filled with harsh images and environments. In one of the song's strongest images, the sun's glinting off of skyscraper windows seems to be setting the world on fire. "we're all rehearsing for the presidency," Ani jests. "i always wanted to be / commander-in-chief / of my one-woman army." It's a refrain we've heard before. But, in the next line, Ani states, "i can envision the mediocrity / of my finest hour / it is the failed america in me." Not without reason, this complex but provocative song is a favorite with Anifans.

Roll With It introduces conga drums like a burst of thunder on a clear day, underscoring the words like aural punctuation marks. At the forefront of the song's imagery lies the stark determination of a man leaving home to go to war (one assumes it's the Gulf War given the release date of the album). "Roll with it" is an often heard refrain, the answer invariably offered up when one asks, "Why are you going to war?" Keep your chin up. Roll with it. But Ani is quick to point up that the men on Capitol Hill made the decisions. Are they worth fighting for? Isn't the "keep America free" rhetoric used as justification for power hunger? Ani begs the man going off to war not to go to the front lines. But, at song's end, the singer admits placidly, "i think my body is as restless / as my mind / and i'm not gonna roll with it this time." Therein lies the song's dramatic impact as we recoil from this odd complacency after such promise of action.

Itch is another woman-leaving-love-behind song, but this time, the images are both anatomical ("i am evening the score / i am cutting the umbilical cord") and geographical ("you can find me crying / on the shoulder / of the road"). "yours was the hardest itch to relieve," the singer admits, an odd sort of praise.

There are times when men don't know the first thing about what it means to be friends with a woman. When the simple act of comforting a woman becomes a request for sex. On *Gratitude* a man offers the singer solace and sanctuary, food and drink as well as a place to stay for the night. The first verse of the song sets the listener up with a series of "thank yous" that culminate in the lines, "thank you / for your half of the bed / we can sleep here like / brother and sister you said." But all too quickly, the singer (and the listener) learn that this series of kindnesses comes with a heavy price tag: "but you changed the rules in an hour or two / / please stop / this is not my obligation / what does my body / have to do / with my gratitude." For the singer, another lesson in keeping up your guard, even when you're at your most vulnerable, another level of disappointment.

A woman awakens in another woman's bed after an evening of intimacy in *The Whole Night*, a song whose deceptively simple power lies in the diametrically opposing viewpoints of the singer. She has a boyfriend, yet allowed a woman into her private world, recalling the power of the event at song's end. One of Ani's finest love songs.

The Next Big Thing, the first of Ani's down-with-the-music-biz songs, sounds, to many of us in the biz, like a catalog of cliches (the exec who's always got a minute or two for the "next big thing," the sleazy club owner who wonders if the chick singer is pretty enough to bring the boys into the bar). The singer is aware of her talent, aware of her ability, not afraid to be herself in the face of the "suits" who want her to "get in the car" and leave behind the small-potatoes scene of playing before a crowd of six people. Ani responds to these invitations to become a star: "and i think / he does not hear / what i'm saying / he's just looking / at my 8x10 / and wondering about / the part that was left out / does she have a body / that will really / draw them in." Ani DiFranco remains loyal to her own vision of how success should be achieved, not surprisingly.

Brief Bus Stop is a snapshot of two women waiting for a bus, but it's also the much broader statement of two women who share similar convictions ("we discovered that we are both / pleasantly furious half the time"), though their means of acting on these convictions differ. While the singer is impatient for change ("i don't know if i can wait / for that peace to be mine"), her bus-stop friend explains her approach through the metaphor of waiting for the bus ("we've been waiting for this bus / for an awfully long time"). Another key element of this song is Ani's portrayal of herself as a storyteller, accepting the burden of articulating the spirit of her generation: "i think we need new responses / every question is a revolving door . . . there will be a new generation of anger / new stories to be told."

In *Looking For The Holes*, Ani does articulate a philosophical position: "you can talk a great philosophy / but if you can't be kind / to people every day / then it doesn't mean much to me / it's the little things you do / it's the little things you say / it's the love you give along the way." Here is Ani's "little people" attitude in full view on a winning number that uses the holes in our clothing as metaphor for the problems in our every day lives. Folk wisdom from a very young folksinger which will be addressed again on her subsequent albums, especially in her collaborations with Utah Phillips.

IMPERFECTLY
(RBR003-D) 1992

What If No One's Watching (3:11)　　*I'm No Heroine* (3:17)
Fixing Her Hair (4:38)　　*Coming Up* (1:46)
In Or Out (3:02)　　*Make Them Apologize* (4:15)
Every State Line (3:03)　　*The Waiting Song* (4:11)
Circle Of Light (2:26)　　*Served Faithfully* (2:50)
If It Isn't Her (3:54)　　*Imperfectly* (3:43)
Good, Bad, Ugly (2:57)

Ani's third album was recorded in early 1992 and included thirteen tracks featuring Ani, drummer Andy Stochansky, and guests Geoff Perry, George Puleo, Tim Allan, and Mary Ramsey. Ramsey had been recruited based on her prior folk-rock recordings as part of Johnny And Mary (which also featured husband John Lombardo). Today, Mary Ramsey fronts 10,000 Maniacs (whose two post-Natalie Merchant releases, LOVE AMONG THE RUINS on Geffen and THE EARTH PRESSED FLAT on Bar/None are recommended). IMPERFECTLY was engineered by Tony Romano and Ed Stone, produced by Ani and Dale at (again) Audio Magic in Buffalo and mastered by Ed Stone. The album is considered something of a classic, earning a four out of five star rating from the *All Music Guide* review collective, a strong follow-up to NOT SO SOFT. Again, Ani's studio chops get more and more acute, the talent easily overpowering any deficiencies (although, I personally found none). The material on IMPERFECTLY covers the usual Ani terrain but with more depth, passion, and greater introspection, all sung in a more confident, more mature voice.

What If No One's Watching, the lead track, starts off in typical Ani fashion: short, sharp, shocked notes while Andy Stochansky's drums and Geoff Perry's bass kick up a storm. "what if no one's watching / what if when we're dead / we are just dead"? asks Ani, getting all metaphysical. "what if god ain't looking down / what if he's looking up instead." The song is a passionate rant, an echo of Ani's soul, and a call to action: "if you're not trying / to make something better / then as far as I'm concerned / you are just in the way."

Fixing Her Hair is another of Ani's snapshot moments which kicks in after a lengthy, laconic introduction to show us Ani and a friend looking into a mirror, fixing their hair, and discussing her friend's lover. While her friend thinks highly of her lover (he's called to apologize, ergo he must be a great guy), Ani sees through this disguise: "i can see her features begin to blur / as she pours herself / into the mold he made for her." An extended metaphor that works as Ani's voice soars higher than usual and Tim Allan's mandolin adds accent.

More hard strumming accompanies *In Or Out*, a song about Ani's sexuality and her answer for people who question it. For her, it isn't about "him/her," "in/out": it's about doing what comes naturally, in the moment, in the now. "some days the line I walk / turns out to be straight / other days the line tends to deviate," Ani sings. At the end, she suggests that a unisexual relationship is like "getting to the same restaurant / and eating the same thing." Just Ani and her guitar, discussing the question in open, unfettered form.

Every State Line comes on like a *fait vecu* song about Ani's experiences on the road. In West Texas she gets pulled over by a state-trooper who's wondering if she's smuggling Mexican immigrants. In Louisiana, she thumbs a ride (after her car breaks down) and gets a sexual come on from the rider. In Alabama she can see everyone staring at her, judging her by her clothes and haircut. In Pennsylvania, the cops ask her to move along after she's parked her car in an empty lot for the night. Ani adds vocal chordings to her chorus. No matter where you go, watch your back. Another recurring Ani-thought — and a nice variation on the classic American open road theme.

Circle Of Light features Greg Horn's trumpet phrases on a no-looking-back number about going towards the center of the circle of light, heading boldly where the future takes you. And while Ani doesn't know what tomorrow may bring, she knows enough not to hang around just outside the light. "i ain't got time for halfway / i ain't got time for half-assed," she states, boldly. This spirit of abandon has endeared her to her fans.

If It Isn't Her contains two strong emotions: her bitter feelings towards a male lover who spurns her and her intense attraction for a woman she meets who comforts her: "honey you are safe here / this is a girl-girl thing." The ambiguity of the situation comes into clear focus when the woman admits that Ani's problems with her beau are boring her. She's just interested in the "girl-girl thing."

Good, Bad, Ugly is a homecoming of sorts as Ani returns home and sees an old boyfriend (and his new girlfriend). Does she still love him? You'd think the answer would be no, until you reach the line: "you know I really didn't intend / to embrace you that long / but then again i noticed / i wasn't the only one hanging on." A common experience sung with considerable depth.

As Ani became the voice of lesbian feminism, the importance placed on her by women looking for larger than life figures to worship thrust her into a larger than life role. One she hated (and still hates).

"i'm no heroine / least not last time i checked," she sings on *I'm No Heroine* in a voice hushed in a vocal equivalent of furrowed eyebrows. Andy Stochansky's drums thud in full sonic wallop, while soaring vocal phrasing acts as bridge between verses. "i don't fool myself like i fool you," Ani states in a wonderful turn of phrase, clearly at odds with the image others project of her.

Coming Up, another recited poem, features Ani's double-tracked vocal gymnastics. And while the double-tracking has strong wordplay, the "row-row-row-your-boat" set-up sometimes detracts from the power of the verses. The final lines are the most telling as Ani states, "whoever's in charge up there / had better take the elevator down / and put more change in our cup or else we /are coming / up."

On *Make Them Apologize*, Ani pillories the patriarchal world. "The music business . . . the marriage business . . . the revolution business" is run by men, none of whom have a clue about the right of a woman to be herself. Ani and Andy's instrumental work swings hard in full, vitriolic fervor.

The Waiting Song is a sensitive, passionate love song portraying a couple trying to live the moments they have together in pure abandon. Ani fights the good fight, hoping that things will "improve, you know they've got to improve" so that they can grow old together. A little too sentimental for Ani DiFranco, perhaps, but saved by a true sense of longing.

On *Served Faithfully*, Mary Ramsey adds beautiful viola phrasings to a song where a woman sees the futility of her relationship with an abusive spouse and tries to recapture a sense of who she is with another man, the return of an old friend. It's probably the purest folk song Ani's written, where you can feel clearly that the emotions came from someone whose personal experience is genuine.

Imperfectly is a fast-paced song about loving one another, well, imperfectly: "let's show them all how it's done / let's do it all imperfectly." Seldom has Ani accepted such limitations in her quest for an ideal relationship. The songs ends the album as it started, with the band adding depth and power to an introspective ballad, creating a sense of empowerment and determination.

PUDDLE DIVE
(RBR004-D) 1993

Names And Dates And Times (2:39)	*Blood In The Boardroom* (3:55)
Anyday (3:00)	*Born A Lion* (1:48)
4th Of July (3:03)	*My IQ* (2:23)
Willing To Fight (3:49)	*Used To You* (3:23)
Egos Like Hairdos (2:44)	*Pick Yer Nose* (2:44)
Back Around (3:09)	*God's Country* (2:50)

There's a marked difference on Ani's fourth album released in 1993. Ani and Dale produced the album at International Sound (still in Buffalo) with Ed Stone engineering yet again. Guests on the album include Ann Rabson, a member of Saffire-The Uppity Blues Women (whose albums are released internationally via Alligator Records), Rory McLeod, a well-respected British blues-harmonica player who has released albums on Cooking Vinyl, and Mary Ramsey. The cover of the album shows us a picture of a young, ecstatic Ani, eyes wide open, smile mischievous, framed in garish yellow/green color with the words "Puddle Dive" in dark tan. Look within and all the song lyrics are written by Ani herself in a scrawl that begs and invites deeper examination. That sense of unbridled joy (and let's be specific here, the kind of joy as experienced by Ani, and *not* a standard, "everything-is-beautiful" kind of joy) is mirrored in the CD booklet photos: Ani in mid-puddle-dive flight, Ani flashing the peace-sign behind a statue of two monkeys, Ani smiling that infamous smile with hands in pockets, looking like a punk Little Rascal. Though I may sound flip writing about her this way, there's no denying the infectious nature of her presence, and on PUDDLE DIVE one really gets the best glimpse of Ani's sly, playful, sardonic nature.

The album is of a piece with the previous IMPERFECTLY and her next album OUT OF RANGE. The three form a potent trilogy which saw her fan base explode towards a younger demographic. The emphasis is on re-contextualizing Ani as a Gen-X folk singer, an alterna-folk punk-rocker whose shocking get-up (not that shocking really) seemed antithetical to the usual folk-singer trappings (no Birkenstocks on her!).

On *Names And Dates And Times*, Brit blues-folk-rocker Rory McLeod plays harmonica and adds a tasty solo on a standard Ani acoustic attack. This is the stuff we like her best for, the ramblings of someone in free-form, stream-of-consciousness fashion: 'i know so many white people / i mean where do i start / the trouble with white people / is you just can't tell them apart." For Ani — on this song at least — most people aren't that remarkable, people who, when offered the chance to speak, say nothing exceptional. Ani challenges these people to say something that'll "wow" her: "why don't you tell me / something i don't already know." But Ani throws this in an ironic tone when she confesses: "i am so many white people / i mean where do i start / i got lots of personalities / i just can't tell them apart." She's everyone and no one, she suggests, not without a sense of playfulness.

On *Anyday*, an introspective Ani tries to look beyond her own short-comings. Everything she does seems wrong, ordinary, average. Her jokes ain't funny any more, and besides, she laughs too much. She's always got her guitar to play but she can do that any day. The touch of ennui that emerges here becomes more pronounced as her career advances.

For *Fourth Of July* Mary Ramsey guests on violin while Ani sings about her encounter with a seven-year-old-boy in an Iowa junkyard. A fast-paced number, the song benefits greatly from Ani's visual eye and her sense of lyrical detail. Jason, out of everyone she's met, doesn't frown at her (her looks being the cause of all the staring). Jason doesn't question, he only smiles, stating he'll be seven on the fourth of July. He lives in the last "trailer on the right." Ani claims he was her only friend in Iowa. A great song filled with vivid imagery and heartfelt emotion.

On *Willing To Fight*, Ani is up on her soapbox again fighting complacency and apathy. "the biggest crime is to throw up your hands," Ani states in angry-acoustic mode, while Andy Stochansky punctuates her words with his drums.

People with overblown egos are the main theme of *Egos Like Hairdos*, a fast-paced song about the difference between a "world of hope" and a "world of hype." Ani rants along in free form about "playing life like it's some stupid sport" and the "cloud of competition that is hanging behind their eyes." Her own ego is examined as she looks to see the print size of her name on the poster advertising her show and where her own name ranks on the artist roster line-up (she's last). A "nyah-nyah-ny-nyah-nyah" chorus adds a touch of necessary silliness, while McLeod blows an upbeat harmonica lick. A sardonic Ani laugh ends the song.

Back Around, a slow, bluesy acoustic song about yet another one night stand in another one-horse town, features Ann Rabson's frames. The song assumes unsettling tones of judgment as Ani sings that she'd rather be anywhere than somewhere hitting a hammer down for ten bucks an hour and selling people shit she wouldn't buy herself for five bucks an hour. The words are drawled out over images of a stifled existence. And the kicker comes from the singer's last sentiments: if she could, she really would stay there. Seldom does Ani cross this line into seeming hypocrisy.

Blood In The Boardroom is Ani's legendary diatribe about the record business, with Scot Fisher's calm accordion creating an ironic atmosphere. Ani gets her period while negotiating with record company brass who feel decidedly uncomfortable about her rather startling announcement. It's a great excuse to escape the men of power and their instruments of death. Ani's disgust with these men is palpable; her response astute. She has the power to create life while the people in the "I'm so bored-room" talk about money and power.

Acoustic guitar strum-attacks kick off *Born A Lion*, another song where Ani makes no apologies for her stance, for speaking her mind, feeling her feelings, and living her life. "i say if you're born a lion / don't bother trying to act tame," Ani sings, a refrain we've heard before, but a refrain we never tire of hearing from Ani because she sings it with such conviction.

On *My IQ* spoken word ramblings are given nuance and shading thanks to Scot Fisher's accompanying accordion. The metaphor for self-examination here is the IQ test, with Ani's score predicting how her life will be lived. But this test never prepared her for the rite of womanhood, never gave her the right tools to become who she is. "every tool is a weapon / if you hold it right," Ani sings.

Used To You seems to be yet another "I-love-him-but-I-hate-him" love song, a fast-paced number where Ani complains about how she's "used to" her current boyfriend and hates him for being "an asshole," yet at the same time, she admits she has a thing for "assholes who talk too much." She bemoans his lack of distinction, his lack of commitment, his apathy. Yet so much of what she sees in him, she's sure exists within herself. By the song's end, she states, "i could love you / yeah i've entertained

116

the thought / but i could never like you / so i guess i'd better not." This admonition, this almost throw-away line, causes the song to turn 180 degrees, serving up a strong image, one filled with power and growth of awareness. Again, it's a standard Ani sentiment, especially in the face of people who are so commonplace. What scares her the most is that she could easily allow herself to fall in love with someone so predictable.

Pick Yer Nose is another rant with Ani wondering why things are the way they are. "who you gonna be / if you can't be yourself," she asks over a flurry of slight polyrhythms (dembe, cuica, samba whistle courtesy Alex Meyer).

What is it with Ani and state-troopers anyway? *God's Country*, an upbeat song with a bouncing rhythm which features Rory McLeod on harmonica, sees our heroine getting pulled over on a prairie highway for speeding. "state trooper thinks I drive too fast / pulled me over to tell me so / i say out here on the prairie / any speed is too slow," Ani states. The country/city dichotomy suits the song well as Ani states she misses Brooklyn (long-time fans will raise an eyebrow and sport a sly smile at the line) and wants to see the country first-hand (because someone had to). Yet she and the trooper share something: that look of righteousness in the face of egress.

LIKE I SAID (SONGS 1990-91)
(RBR005-D) 1993

Anticipate (2:42)	*Both Hands* (3:01)
Rockabye (4:01)	*She Says* (3:36)
Not So Soft (3:01)	*Rush Hour* (4:50)
Roll With It (3:22)	*Out Of Habit* (2:32)
Work Your Way Out (3:40)	*Lost Woman Song* (4:00)
Fire Door (2:57)	*Talk To Me Now* (3:57)
Gratitude (2:44)	*The Slant* (1:45)
The Whole Night (2:20)	

For her fifth album, Ani re-worked many songs from her first two albums to include percussion and slight instrumental shadings. Ani's surer vocal delivery also adds more depth to material that may have seemed tentative. Tracks like *Roll With It* benefit the most from the re-workings (cool trumpet licks add accent) thanks to strong production and detailed space in the remakes. A cello adds nuance and shading to *Work Your Way Out*.

She Says features subtle (!!) bagpipes. *Talk To Me Now* adds steady, beat-ready drumming, and while that might have spelt out certain doom for the words, the nuances are subtle enough to underscore and not over-ride. What emerges is a strong collection of songs, numbers Ani still performs at shows and concerts. Too subtle to be a "greatest hits" collection, it's a skilled attempt at broadening her fan base by recasting the earlier songs in a "younger" language. The first two albums had received limited distribution and attention came primarily from two camps: the folk community and women's rights groups (specifically lesbian/gay communities). By recasting her earlier material in a "younger" sounding music, Ani's increasing fan-base (which, in all honesty, had always had college/university support as well) became acquainted with the past canon in a readily accessible fashion. For Ani, the time probably seemed right to revisit the past and give it the kind of lustre she may have wished it had originally. And as Ani increased the sound of her concerts to include the musicians she used as back-up singers, it only seemed natural to take a side trip down memory lane, as it were (thereby allowing the musicians to get a real hold on the older material). Yet the cover art comes from Ani's past: the serious folk singer holding a guitar as big as she is, kneeling in a room devoid of accoutrement and furniture. It's a stark, black and white photo that might have seemed to some (especially those from the folk community who had written her off) as a swan song of sorts. As if this part of her existence had come to an end and was being acknowledged with a funereal kind of send-off. But at the core of the release comes the strength of the material itself, resilient and elastic, announcing the coming of age of a singer in total control of her image and attitude. Whatever the reason for the release, it made good sense and continues to cast magic over the DiFranco catalog.

OUT OF RANGE
(RBR006-D) 1994

Building And Bridges (4:00)	*Face Up And Sing* (2:50)
Out Of Range (acoustic) (3:43)	*Falling Is Like This* (2:57)
Letter To A John (3:44)	*Out Of Range (electric)* (3:22)
Hell Yeah (4:57)	*You Had Time* (5:45)
How Have You Been (4:25)	*If He Tries Anything* (3:12)
Overlap (3:41)	*The Diner* (4:39)

By 1994, Ani's career had settled into a winning groove as concerts took her to larger venues and a higher profile on the alternative circuit brought higher sales, especially of the like sounding three albums IMPERFECTLY, PUDDLE DIVE, and OUT OF RANGE, her 'mid-career' trilogy. Recorded and produced in December of 1993, OUT OF RANGE marks the first time Ani and engineer Ed Stone worked outside of Buffalo. The album was recorded at 1:2:1 Recording Studios in Toronto with final mastering occurring at The Lacquer Channel in the Toronto suburb of Scarborough. Ani designed the album art and Scot Fisher contributed photos. Ani hands out heart-felt thank yous on the album, giving due acknowledgment to Dale Anderson, the people at Fleming/Tamulevich (her booking agency), and her parents, among others.

The album is a sure-footed traverse across rockier terrain, both lyrical and musical. The themes are direct, unflinching and uncompromising, while the pop music is muscular, detailed, fine-tooled, and emotional. Over the course of its twelve tracks, the listener (especially the listener familiar with previous releases) feels that there is a sense of fulfilment about OUT OF RANGE. The narrow strip of road photographed on the front cover might seem like a narrow path ahead, but the voice, music, and production aspire to deep introspection. On OUT OF RANGE, Ani achieves just that.

The album features two versions of the title track, one acoustic, the other electric. Maybe it was the Neil Young (*My My Hey Hey*) influence that led her to recast the song in this fashion. Yet the album seems a trifle too sure of itself, too comfortable with the folk-trappings and her standard themes. While OUT OF RANGE has much of the same musical muscle as PUDDLE DIVE and IMPERFECTLY, it doesn't have the stark, alternative-music look and sound of NOT A PRETTY GIRL, DILATE, and LITTLE PLASTIC CASTLE (or UPX6 for that matter). The songs have an air of finality about them, with a suggestion that the cocoon had been ruptured and something altogether different was emerging. Ani would re-invent herself on NOT A PRETTY GIRL a year later.

On *Buildings And Bridges*, Ani seems in full control of image, sound, lyric, production and ability. The lead track to her sixth album features bass (Alisdair Jones) and drums (Andy Stochansky) fleshing out an introspective lyric. The melody isn't harsh or biting, the singer instead opting for a fluid style that sounds more akin to the standard folk songs she had sung in the past. Ani addresses people who would typecast her (were they expecting a "bitch"?), while not considering that like buildings and bridges, she bends to the wind.

Out Of Range (Acoustic) presents us with so many standard Ani images in one song that the net effect encapsulates her career. There are three main metaphors at work here: the complacency of a woman in a no-win relationship who has found the power of flight; the righteousness of defending one's position in a political arena ("when the men of the hour / can kill half the world in war"); and the dread of being locked up in an image not of her choosing or making (being her mother's daughter, "thinking nothing ever changes"). For Anifans, the first two sound like common enough sentiments, ones we're used to hearing. But the mother/ daughter imagery is a powerful undercurrent to the way the singer tries to stay just "out of range" of what's expected ("if you drive you / just gotta drive / out of range"). By staying "out of range," the singer hopes to remain true to herself, true to her world, her vision, her very existence. The lyrics are strong with sharp visual images: walls being punched by her lover just beside Ani's head, the Apocalypse, starving oneself to retain control over motherly dominance. The three images at the core of the song's structure create powerful statements and the breadth of the concept comes across in a way that recalls the finer moments of classic folk-rock lyricism. Think of Joni Mitchell's *Both Sides Now*, Jackson Browne's *The Fuse*, or Bob Dylan's *Blowin' In The Wind*, just to name three.

On *Letter To A John* Ani looks at life through the eyes of a lap-dancer/prostitute, one of the few moments in her song catalog where she assumes a voice not her own. For the prostitute, this is just business, just a matter of making money: "i want you to pay me for my beauty / i think it's only right / 'cause I've been paying for it all of my life." Strong images dominate (the prostitute being taken at the age of eleven, giving up something she didn't even know she had). Yet never once does Ani condemn either the 'john' or the 'pro'. When the song's narrator says "i'm gonna take my money and run away," the listener fears this will never happen. Electric guitar adds tension, making the song one of the few out-and-out rockers Ani has written. Yet at the core of the song's imagery is the uncomfortable way Ani sings the lyric about being taken as an eleven year old. The lyric rings with an authenticity that questions the song's imaginary landscape. Of all Ani's songs, this one makes the listener restless, not because there is truth in the vision, but because the woman singing the song has so much despair, in direct contrast to the *hope* for her own future, that the listener is humbled by the parting words: "i'm gonna take and i'm gonna go away."

Hell Yeah offers hushed acoustic pop on an unrequited love song with some memorable lines and rhymes: "life is a B-movie / it's stupid and it's strange / it's a directionless story / and the dialogue is lame / but in the he said she said / sometimes there's some poetry." In another verse she admits, "i was a terrible waitress so i started writing songs." At root, the song is another story about how she loves him but can't talk to him about it. Barriers exist. They are mute.

On *How Have You Been*, soul horns and a saxophone punctuate a fast-paced funk-rocker about the meeting of two ex-lovers. It's Ani at her soulful best, the words full of bite and spittle (yet never, ever sounding confrontational). Ani's yearning for the past manifests itself in questionable fashion as she admits she doesn't want to be near him and his new girlfriend, but will be watching by the window come night-time. It's another "forbidden fruit" song whose image, framed in the form of the "how have you been ?" question, leaves the listener wary of the sad state of affairs when love and its dark side entrap someone who cannot break free of its grip.

So many of Ani's songs use irony as underpinning for the way two people feel about each other. *Overlap* seems to be a love song of sorts until Ani states, matter-of-factly: "either you don't have the balls / or you don't feel the same." Ani and her guitar keep things direct and simple, at least on a musical level.

The lyric "it's nice that you listen / it'd be nicer if you joined in" from *Face Up And Sing* has become a fave DiFranco line expressing Ani's expectations of her audience and their expectations of her. Ani's ambivalence towards her audience is clear: "some chick says / thank you for saying all the things i never do / i say you know the thanks i get / is to take all the shit for you." A lovely, witty upbeat pop tune featuring Scot Fisher on accordion.

Falling Like This is another ballad about failing to live up to personal expectations: "i'm sorry i can't help you / i cannot keep you safe / sorry i can't help myself / so don't look at me that way."

Out Of Range (Electric) is a rockier version of the second track. There's a definite Springsteen aura to the song (thanks to backing vocal wails) that makes it a more urgent sounding cry to arms than the acoustic version.

On *You Had The Time* ambling piano opens the song, after which a guitar enters, muted and quiet, taking up the melody. Ani sings again about meeting a long-distance lover: "how can i go home / with nothing to say." The piano seems at odds with the singer's laconic mood as Ani recognizes she must move on.

Another powerful ballad, *If He Tries Anything* shows feminine companionship at work in a sisterly way as two friends share life experiences, lovers, themselves. Each would protect the other: they both carry switchblades in their sleeves. "i'll be watching you from the wings / i will come to your rescue / if he tries anything."

Background sounds and a count-off open *The Diner* which adds clinking china plates to the percussion. Someone phones an ex-lover (late at night) and begs for company (with mocking laughter underscoring the true feelings of the caller). At the song's end, the caller states they'll wait there for the ex-lover until the coffee runs cold, but you know the ex-lover will never come. Ambient conversation ends the disc.

NOT A PRETTY GIRL
(RBR007-D) 1995

Worthy (4:31)	*The Million You Never Made* (4:18)
Tiptoe (0:36)	*Hour Follows Hour* (6:01)
Cradle And All (4:18)	*32 Flavors* (6:07)
Shy (4:43)	*Asking Too Much* (2:55)
Sorry I Am (4:45)	*This Bouquet* (2:28)
Light Of Some Kind (4:07)	*Crime For Crime* (5:42)
Not A Pretty Girl (3:55)	*Coming Up* (2:29)

NOT A PRETTY GIRL, the first album which sported the current Righteous Babe Records logo (of a woman flexing her muscles in a proud, defiant stance), was recorded at The Record Complex in Buffalo and at 1:2:1 in

Toronto in 1995. Ed Stone returned for the engineering duties, while Tom Heron and Mark Peters assisted. George Graves handled the mastering, Mark Dellas contributed photos. Ani designed the cover art herself. This was the first record to not contain Dale Anderson's presence, and the first record to mention "Goat Boy" (known here as Goatie), a.k.a. Andy Gilchrist. Ani and Andy Stochansky shared musical accompaniment duties (with Kate Fenner adding backing vocals on *Asking Too Much*).

NOT A PRETTY GIRL seems to mark the end of an era in Ani's career and look forward to the next. This was the last album before the Alanis Morissette era began with the inevitable comparisons. For Ani, the album marked a return to some of the folk motifs she'd used to make her first two albums so endearing. It's perhaps her most fully realized album, one where all the elements flow perfectly in total synchronicity. The music, usually Ani on guitar with drummer Andy Stochansky, is a heady mix of folk, punk, and rock, both modern and acoustic. Ani's voice is a powerful instrument, lashing out where needed, muted and breathless when called for. NOT A PRETTY GIRL is the culmination of her earliest recordings and the promise of the future. For many fans, this album embodies what makes Ani great.

Backward tape effects start off *Worthy*, then Ani's voice soars in fuller form on a song about not being good enough in this world: "you think you're not worthy / i'd have to say i agree / i'm not worthy of you / you're not worthy of me." But through it all, maybe, by being together they can be worthy of each other.

A fast-paced, machine-gun spoken word attack sets *Tiptoe* off, a song that portrays a woman wrestling with her decision to have an abortion: "tiptoeing thru the used condoms . . . with a fetus holding court in my gut / my body hijacked . . . i could step off the end of this pier but I got / shit to do / and an appointment next tuesday / to shed uninvited blood and tissue." The wordplay is perfect, setting up troubling images and locations, intense emotions and ideas. The song offers an abject lesson in trying to overturn stereotypes. As Ani explains in the book *Solo*, "When I was recording it, there were these really funny outtakes. The poem begins with me walking across the room to the microphone, but in my sneakers, the footsteps weren't loud enough, so I borrowed my friend Ed's boots, which are twice the size of my feet. I started walking across the room in the pitch black because I always record in the dark. So I'm clomping through the studio, tripping over things and laughing hysterically. I put those outtakes on the album because they were so funny, but several people asked me, as if they were addressing Satan Woman, how I could be talking about an abortion and laughing. I should have the personal freedom to react emotionally without having my response restricted or dictated by anyone else. Don't tell me I have to be somber because I'm reading an abortion poem." Sometimes the soap box becomes slippery.

The acoustic guitar lines on *Cradle And All* come right off of the word "back" on *Tiptoe*. This fast-paced folk rocker accents another slice-of-life-since-I-moved-to-NYC lyric, its title a continuation of *Rockabye*, with an image of Ani's uncle, unemployed after a factory shutdown, "standing out in the cold," being told to "have fun growing old," while the refrain of "down will fall baby, cradle and all" threatens her life. "take me home / take me home and leave me there," she pleads, "think I'm gonna cry / don't know why / think I'm gonna sing myself a lullaby."

Drums and bass propel *Shy* forward, the lyrics a morning-after confessional (a startled hotel chamber-maid departs upon discovering the narrator and "friend" in bed) where the singer begs to be stopped if she starts to sink into cliches. *Shy* is beloved by Ani fans (and a personal favorite of mine as well, nominated for a Grammy award in the live version on LIVING IN CLIP.) Strong within/without imagery prevails. Within, the sheets are wet from love-making and heat. Without, far-away-in-the-city, "the men are pissing in doorways / and the rats are running in herds." But there's a desperate quality to Ani's voice when she sings the chorus, "you'll stop me won't you / if you've heard this one before," the despair which comes from falling in way too deep while keeping an ever-wary eye on the nearest exit.

Sorry I Am is a hushed ballad filled with remorse for love unrequited, with a twist as the singer apologizes to her lover for not loving him or her as much as she was loved: "i guess i never loved you quite as well / as the way you loved me / i guess i'll never be able to tell you / how sorry i am." A deeply compassionate reversal of a standard love song.

On *Light Of Some Kind*, short, clipped, stuttering notes plucked from Ani's guitar accentuate the song's lyric. A woman admits infidelity to her boyfriend (the indiscretion stems from an affair with another woman).

"maybe you should follow / my example / and go meet yourself / a really nice girl," Ani states in urgent, clipped, gulped words, one of Ani's most resonant lines, a bold declaration of both Ani's infidelity and her regret for the mediocrity of the relationship. Again, there is desperation in the song's chorus, Ani's urgent tone a symbol of yearning for the "truth" in any relationship: "cuz at the end of this tunnel / of guilt and shame / there must be a light of some kind / give me a light of some kind / i want a light of some kind."

The angry folk rock song *Not A Pretty Girl* lambastes people who perceive Ani as being something she is not ("a damsel in distress or a kitten stuck up a tree"). People fail to realize she can help herself out of any trouble, that she has been "fighting the good fight." A passionate song about the power of the individual in the face of criticism, expectation, and ideology, *Not A Pretty Girl* is Ani's declaration of independence which has given the same sense of freedom to many of her fans.

The Million You Never Made is one of Ani's harshest anti-record-industry songs, its portrayal of a promo rep scathing, probably based on someone Ani met in the business. Again, staccato guitar notes add punctuation to her judgmental words as Ani states that he's wrong if he thinks he has her pegged: "you can dangle your carrot / but i ain't gonna reach for it / cuz i need both hands / to play my guitar." The band kicks in for the bridge as Ani sees right through the promo haze. Kick drums punch out the lead to the final verse where Ani proudly proclaims (in Who-styled strummed guitars) that "she could be the million that you never made." This song remains one of her fans faves thanks to its "ain't gonna take it and ain't gonna give it away" attitude.

Hour Follows Hour is another introspective ballad where true love escapes: "maybe we are both good people / who've done some bad things / . . . i hope in the end we can laugh and say / it was all worth it." The song has one of the truest lines about love lost: "too much is how i love you / but too well is how i know you."

32 Flavors shows Ani as her own person, subject to the expectations of no one, in an upbeat number with soft touches and sure vocals. Just a standard folk-rock ballad about not pinning any one down. "i am 32 flavors and then some," she states as drums fade the song to the end. When Alana Davis released her version, she rewrote some of the words, removing the song's dark underpinnings. "Ani is very much her own songwriter, you know, and I think of her songs as being very specific to her ideals and stuff," Davis told *MTV News* in February 1998. "At first I wasn't sure about taking her ideas and trying to make them my own and re-interpreting them. But I started to play around with it . . . I took out the parts that I wasn't comfortable with and I put in ideas of my own and sent her a copy of it and she said she loved it, so. . . ." Fans soon grew to hate Davis' version as the song rose high atop Billboard's Top 100 Singles charts, but many Anifans don't realize Ani was fine with Davis' version, wrongly thinking she was somehow "done wrong" by Davis. It didn't help that Davis, whose album was a debut for a major label, attracted huge sales. Davis seemed not to have paid her dues. At the heart of Davis's interpretation lies her love for the song's tone, image, structure, and power, which makes her version a fine pop song in the traditional sense of the word. Ani's version, with her nervous, angered wordplay, has none of Davis's pop finish. Its passion lies in the unexpected: if life is 32 flavors, she's more than that. Sung in Ani's unforgettable manner, her *32 Flavors* outdistances Davis's by many, many miles.

On *Asking Too Much*, a double-time waltz supports Ani's stream-of-consciousness wish list for qualities in a friend/lover/partner/significant other, with the final line asking, playfully, "do you think I'm asking too much?"

Ani sings, "seems like I'm starving for words whenever you're around," as she plucks some words from the "garden" of thoughts in her mind on *This Bouquet*, a beautiful, acoustic song filled with quiet, introspective voice and guitar work.

Crime For Crime is a moody folk-rocker about the "hanging" of justice, the trading of crime for crime, no matter who and what you are, of judging and condemning somebody for their beliefs before understanding them. At the core of the song's lyric lies the sense that Ani owes nothing to anyone, especially those who've condemned her without looking at all the facts in her life. It could just as easily be about the anger she feels at being judged by the lesbian, folk, or womyn's movement communities. There is a sense of doom at play as the song's narrative unfolds. The singer has been condemned and is being executed. The eleventh hour brings remorse from the singer ("i went too far and i'm sorry / i guess now i'm going home"). But don't you believe for one moment that the singer is begging for forgiveness. It just isn't her style.

Coming Up is another of Ani's patented stream of consciousness word-plays, the metaphors flying fast and furious, seemingly "coming up" for air, tackling the futility of believing in a religion that seems uncaring, feeling the despair of unrequited passion, facing the menace of an overbearing government in total loss of control. "but i love this city, this state / this country is too large / and whoever is in charge up there / had better take the elevator down / and put more change in our cup / or else we / are coming / up." All accented by plunking percussion touches and electric piano. The song ends 1:45 before the end. Then, Ani adds three, uncredited, flubbed "outtakes" of *Tiptoe*.

DILATE
(RBR008-D) 1996

Untouchable Face (4:38)	*Shameless* (4:51)
Outta Me, Onto You (4:35)	*Done Wrong* (6:31)
Superhero (4:45)	*Done Wrong* (6:31)
Dilate (4:48)	*Adam And Eve* (6:37)
Amazing Grace (7:07)	*Joyful Girl* (5:04)
Napoleon (6:24)	

Recorded in December 1995 and January 1996, DILATE features more trademark Ani-songs with drummer Andy. Three studios were used: Congress House Studio in Austin, Texas; Grant Avenue Studio in Hamilton, Ontario; Chemical Sound in Toronto. Mark Hallman, Marty Lester, and Ed Stone handled duties in Austin, while Bob Doidge and Robin Aube took care of duties in Hamilton. Andy Gilchrist was present for the Toronto portion. Ani mixed the stuff herself in Texas with Chris Bellman handling mastering duties at L.A.'s Bernie Grundman Mastering. Again, Ani designed the album (with credited help from Adam Pause). Eye-pupils dilate. The female cervix dilates as it prepares for birth. Two possible interpretations come to mind. Does the title refer to the widening and narrowing of Ani's cinematic, inner eye? Or to Ani's rebirth as an alterna-rock, post-riot grrl folkster?

Part of what makes DILATE succeed so well is the presence of Andy S.,

Ani's erstwhile and supportive drummer. His presence is felt more acutely on this release. Other guests include David Travers-Smith on trumpet and Michael Ramos on organ. Everything else is handled by Andy'n'Ani. The cover shows the L'il Folksinger kneeling, face hidden by blue-dyed corn-rowed hair, hands nail-polished black. The word "dilate" appears in faded white letters, dominating the CD cover, almost as if she were deliberately keeping her face hidden.

Critics and reporters often categorize DILATE as Ani's "coming out of the gay closet and into the straight one" album, the songs apparently turning off a large contingent of her "queer" following based on the he/she nature of the lyrics. But the lyrics are ambiguous, deliberately so, it would seem, allowing the listeners to bring their own interpretation to the songs based on their own subjective experience. This freedom of interpretation makes these songs sparkle and succeed. DILATE turned out to be break-through album for Ani. Younger fans flocked to its words and music in the wake of media attention following Alanis Morissette's breakthrough with JAGGED LITTLE PILL. Long-time, older Anifans saw the album as another stage in her evolution as a mature artist.

Reunions, especially with former lovers, hold much power in our lives. At the back of the mind is the niggling question of reconciliation, though most times, that never happens. *Untouchable Face* presents the listener with just such a scenario as Ani bears her soul to a former lover. A trumpet underpins everything like a foghorn blowing a warning. The chorus of "fuck you and your untouchable face" sounds like both an admonition and a sly smile, a sense of ambivalence that makes the song powerful, its words more than just the cheap cuss of a bitter "babe" long-ing for her lover's return. The world is far too complex for that. The thrill, for the listener, is trying to figure out the meaning of the "fuck you" word-play at the core of the song's chorus.

Outta Me, Onto You is Led Zepp's *Your Time Is Gonna Come* for Gen-x'ers. Grunge-like folk-punk dominates as two voices yell "no! no! no!" at the song's start. Ani's mad and promises to tear a strip offa that sucka! The words are spat out with venom and bile: "don't think 'cuz i'm easy, i'm naive / don't think i won't pull it out / don't think i won't shoot." But the song returns to the overriding Ani sentiment, "i'm gonna miss you when you're gone / yeah i'm gonna be torn / just remember that i love you / just remember you were warned."

Superhero features an acoustic beginning and brush-stroke drumming as Ani talks about no longer being a superhero to her lesbian audience. "if I did my tricks with smoke and mirrors / would you know which one is me?" Ani asks. "i'm just like everybody else," she sings (as if that were the end of everything even though it isn't). Muted phone booth voice leads to full vocal (as if she were distancing herself from it all). This is one of her finest songs with its deft guitar work, tight ensemble support, and intense word-play. It's probably what Lucifer sang as he fell from heaven after being cast out.

Severe strums showcase another you-let-me-down song on *Dilate* as Ani spits out her words of release. The musical bridge features loud drum kicks and a wailing Hammond organ. "i'm better, i'm better, i'm better off . . . alone," she sings, almost swallowing the words. Her voice soars at the end, the anguished angel released from the torment. It's an emotion we've heard time and again from Ani, yet it still sounds fresh and original, menacing and vibrant.

Amazing Grace is the ultimate in DIY recording as Ani plays everything while reprising the old gospel standard using alt-dance trappings (sampled voices, electronic sounding drums and percussion, muted vocal effects). The song's religious message is transformed into a spiritual awakening. A sampled voice admits being saved by the rapture of Christ, but recast in this context, this becomes the voice of everywoman in the face of an unfeeling world. Acoustic slide guitar work overcomes the sampled words, demeaning them into rhythm and robbing them of their power. A sampled motorcycle engine revving underpins the return to the first verse. Bells sound off in the song's closing minutes. A Hammond organ gives the cover some of that old-time-religion feel, while muted Ani vocals try to keep control over the returning sampled voice, creating an intense moment of introspection from the song's rapture.

Just who is the subject of *Napoleon*, another of Ani's infamous anti-rock-biz songs? Is it a contemporary of hers? Or is it Ani herself, seeing a reflection of what she could become? The question begs asking because so much of what Ani has written with regards to the subject in the past sees her confronting the industry and emerging triumphant, in total control of her image and talents. But look at the song from the angle of someone else and the singer notices that this other performer is surrounded by suits and the money, the "biz" and all its trappings, and hopes that the performer is happy. "everyone is a fucking napoleon," she sings, almost judging the performer for having chosen that path. History students will recall Napoleon's delusions of grandeur and determination to control a magnificent empire. She resents the one-hour phone call from the performer who calls to bellyache about how things are. "how dare you complain to me," sings Ani, a serious accusation of sell-out from a woman who kept total control, even in the face of not making the millions the performer has now achieved. "Now that you're a big star, do you miss the earth?" asks Ani in a condemning tone. Could Ani be talking about herself and what she could become? Sometimes, imagining the extreme of a given situation brings one renewed vigor and insight. To see yourself as an Elvis Presley-type "icon-of-your-generation" may be easy, but to strive every day for righteous action is much harder, as Ani has told us before.

A false start leads to a strummed introduction on *Shameless*. Bullhorn vocals sing/speak of the singer's shamelessness as she comes on to another woman in search of a sexual relationship. "i gotta cover my butt 'cuz i covet / another man's wife," she sings in this lusty song. Anguished drumming overtakes the song in the middle, bridging it to the final chorus: "say i was shameless / . . . . / and say you just hung around / 'cuz you couldn't stop it." Seldom has Ani sounded so "shameless" about her sexual desires.

On *Done Wrong* Ani accuses her lover of twice abandoning her: "how could you take almost everything / and then come back for the rest." The music swirls like the wind and rain around the narrator as she questions her lover, and the chorus is repeated as Ani lets her angry, anguished voice soar higher towards the end of each line.

Many Anifans respond in loud fashion when Ani sings the words "mister limp dick" on *Going Down*, ridiculing a lover who's "up to his old tricks." Ani recites the words in detached fashion, almost robotically. "you are going down," the singer states so calmly and coldly as to send shivers up and down the spine.

Adam And Eve is the story of a somewhat sordid one-night stand: "tonight you stooped to my level / i am your mangy little whore / . . . / but i know it's 'cuz you think you're adam / and i'm eve." And while Ani doesn't criticize or condemn the event, she begs the lover not to say she was something that "happened" to him. She's wide-eyed enough to know the routine: "i just happen to like apples / and i'm not afraid of snakes."

Look deep into the heart of *Joyful Girl* and you'll see an image of the singer crying, crying because of the way she's been mistaken and misjudged by people all around her who "mostly get it wrong." She sings for joy: "i do it for the joy it brings / because i'm a joyful girl / because the world owes me nothing / and we owe each other the world." A beautiful sentiment expressed simply, passionately, humbly.

LIVING IN CLIP
(RBR011-D) 1997

CD 1:

Whatever	*I'm No Heroine*
[Albuquerque, NM] (1:47)	[Berkeley, CA] (4:16)
Wherever [Santa Ana, CA] (0:07)	*Amazing Grace* [Buffalo, NY] (6:18)
Gravel [New London, CT] (4:12)	*Anticipate* [Ithaca, NY] (3:48)
Willing To Fight	*Tiptoe*
[Sacramento, CA] (4:13)	[N/A] (0:38)
Shy [Houston, TX] (4:29)	*Sorry I Am* [New York, NY] (4:47)
Joyful Girl	*The Slant/The Diner*
[Eugene, OR] (4:26)	[Atlanta, GA] (8:23)
Hide And Seek	*32 Flavors*
[Hightstown, NJ] (4:34)	[Boulder, CO] (4:48)
Napoleon	*Out Of Range*
[Northhampton, MA] (4:54)	[Portland, OR] (4:27)

CD 2:

Untouchable Face	*Not So Soft*
[Bloomington, IL] (3:36)	[New York, NY] (4:00)
Shameless [Portland, OR] (4:35)	*Travel Tips* [Spokane, WA] (1:05)
Distracted	*Wrong With Me*
[San Francisco, CA] (1:08)	[Ithaca, NY] (1:57)
Adam And Eve	*In Or Out*
[New York, NY] (5:36)	[New York, NY] (3:22)
Fire Door	*We're All Gonna Blow*

[Worcester, MA] (4:03)   [Victoria, BC] (2:41)
Both Hands   *Letter To A John*
[Buffalo, NY] (4:50)   [San Francisco, CA] (3:57)
Out Of Habit   *Overlap*
[Arcafa, CA] (3:40)   [New York, NY] (5:57)
Every State Line [Atlanta, GA] (3:55)

Although the CD doesn't mention any concert dates, most of the material recorded on LIVING IN CLIP comes from 1996 and features Ani's concert and touring unit: Ani on acoustic guitar and vocals (and bass on *Hide And Seek*); Andy Stochansky on drums, percussion, backing vocals and harmonica; ex-Gang of Four/League of Gentlemen bassist Sara Lee on bass, bass pedals, and backing vocals. Andy Gilchrist and Ani mixed the album at The Congress House in Austin, Texas in 1997. On *Amazing Grace* and *Both Hands*, Ani is accompanied by The Buffalo Philharmonic Orchestra, conducted by Doc Severinsen and arranged by James Mabry.

If her studio albums leave her slightly disappointed with the recording process, then her live album celebrates the raw and undiluted side of Ani. Indeed, this album captures the L'il Folksinger in fine, joyous mode. The songs achieve a larger than life hue thanks to the intensity of Stochansky's drumming and Lee's driving bass. Ani's words sound urgent and clipped, full and menacing, proper yet immediate. The recordings, captured on ADAT using an 8-track mixing console, give the singer and band room to move without clinical proceedings. Audience sounds are captured by Ani's vocal microphone (and seemed to come from the first ten rows), but the direct non-miking of the audience (a technique so prevalent with rock concert performance recordings) allows the intensity of Ani's live performances to be heard unfettered. Many of the performances gain added perspective and power, especially *Shy* which attracted a Grammy Award nomination. The CD box includes a 32-page 'family' photo album, where we see for the first time members of the band and manager Scot Fisher posing and acting out for the camera, as well as action shots of Ani performing on tour. The liner sleeve notes give a definition of "Clipping an Amp," suggesting the spirit of Living in Clip: "Overloading an amplifier with a sonic signal that exceeds the machine's power capacity, resulting in a terrifying snapping sound and the illumination of a tiny red warning light on the face of the amp indicating that it is about to blow."

Critics were quick to call LIVING IN CLIP the definitive Ani recording. For those wanting to hear a complete image of Ani as she appears on any given night on any given tour, the album has no peer. As a seminal live album, LIVING IN CLIP shares equal billing with the ROYAL ALBERT HALL concert of Bob Dylan, FRAMPTON COMES ALIVE by '70s rocker Peter Frampton, and Joni Mitchell's MILES OF AISLES.

LITTLE PLASTIC CASTLE
(RBR012-D) 1998

Little Plastic Castle (4:03)	*Loom* (2:51)
Fuel (4:01)	*Pixie* (4:25)
Gravel (3:32)	*Swan Dive* (6:28)
As Is (4:06)	*Glass House* (5:18)
Two Little Girls (4:57)	*Independence Day* (3:44)
Deep Dish (3:38)	*Pulse* (14:16)

For LITTLE PLASTIC CASTLE, Ani and Andy returned to Texas and The Congress House studio with the team of Marty Lester, Mark Hallman, and Bob Doidge in full tow. Ani had previously performed *Gravel* (which appeared on LIVING IN CLIP) and *Independence Day* in concert before finally committing them to a studio-recorded release. Her touring band, dubbed The Traveling Circus, appear on many of the tracks. Present with Mr. DiFranco are Jason Mercer on bass, Andy Stochansky (yet again) on drums, John Mills on baritone ska, Gary Slechta on trumpet, Jon Blondell on trombone, Sara Lee on bass, studio drummer Jerry Marotta, Andy the Goat Boy himself on pump organ, and ambient trumpet legend Jon Hassell. As usual, Ani and Adam Sloan handled lay-out duties, while the computer generation "tomfoolery" was courtesy of Albert Sanchez.

Critics were quick to praise LITTLE PLASTIC CASTLE as a work of full-bodied instrumentation and direct emotional power, a far cry from Ani's "just a guitar and l'il ol' me" beginnings. The playfulness of the album's graphics is reflected in the singer's sure-voiced lyrics and music, more so than on any other album. The band sounds full, warm, and comfortable with one another. The ensemble performances are filled with taut compassion, and the word-play is steeped in images, atmospheres, and colored hues not heard on any of Ani's previous albums. One has to peel back the layers of thought here to get at the kernels of truth. The lyrics are less transparent, more complex.

If Ani's lesbian coterie had felt abandoned by DILATE, then Ani showed no signs of this on the album's lead title track as she portrays a lesbian couple meeting at a coffee shop "which is every coffee shop in every city . . . every day"), while the regulars' "sneer at the two girls from out of town." A fat-sounding horn section blurts notes out triumphantly as the singer defends her own image ('people talk / about my image / like i come in two dimensions") and pokes fun at the gawking regulars ("i wish they could see us now / in leather bras and rubber shorts"). Again, there's a slightly dark cloud on this laconic landscape.

Fuel is a poetic complaint serving up a stream of consciousness set of apocalyptic lyrics delivered in an immediate yet slightly paranoid voice that sounds like its owner will snap any second. The song is a fragile, fractured, frightened laugh. The world may end — and she knows it: "beneath the good and the bad and the kind and the stupid and the cruel / there's a fire that's just waiting for fuel."

To some, the illusion of freedom is a powerful aphrodisiac, a dominant emotion that overwhelms the decision making process. The woman portrayed in *Gravel* faces this question. She knows her relationship with her male lover is a stagnant one, knows he's yet another "mister limp dick" cheating on her behind her back. But because he owns a motorcycle and is riding it with him to Californ-eye-aye, the woman continues to remain in this dead-end relationship. Ani delivers the words in her own, well-known staccato/punctuated phrasing: "so let's go before i change my mind / i'll leave the luggage of all your lies behind."

As Is is the mirror image of *Gravel*. Here, the song's heroine knows she's in a go-nowhere relationship but takes him "as is," fully conscious of her decision: "when i look around / i think this, this is good enough / and i try to laugh / at whatever life brings." Placed in the context of Ani's collected works, the sense of irony here is inescapable, as she seems to be feeling the exact opposite of what the character in the song says.

Two Little Girls starts off as a "day in the life of Ani" song as she recalls the great days of a lesbian relationship (brought about by a reunion of the two). While she resents the friend's current lover ("i loved you first"), we learn the reason why the relationship ended. In a harrowing chorus (perhaps the harshest visual image she's ever painted) Ani sings, "here comes little naked me padding up to the bathroom door / to find little naked you slumped on the bathroom floor / so I guess I'll just stand here with my back against the wall / while you distil your whole life down to a 911 call." Strummed guitar chords fade out as the words turn from warm remembrances to bitter accusations of betrayal and loss.

Horns kick up a reggae tinged ditty about yet another night in a bar fighting off the advances of oh-so-boring men on *Deep Dish*, a bleak vision of the club world Ani has portrayed better before.

On *Loom*, a woman tries to make friends with a man who is married ("i won't do anything / you can't tell your wife"), asking him to remove the "dark sunglasses" that always got "between us when we talk," tempting him into her confidence with a challenge ("just try to be as brave as our songs") and a promise ("i will bring my heart / i will bring my face / you name the time and place"). A strong song about stripping away pretences and finding the courage to be a friend: "i want a monument of the friendship / . . . / i want it to take up lots of room / i want it to loom."

Things are not always what they seem to be on *Pixie*. The singer may be a pixie, but she clearly resents it. Haunted downward vocal soars give the song a slightly sinister hue. Sara Lee's bass bounces along in like fashion, accenting the word-play: " 'cuz i'm a pixie / i'm a paper doll / i'm a cartoon / i'm a chipper cheerful free for all. . . ."

Swan Dive is a rare song of triumph, not unlike *Joyful*, though tempered with a touch of weariness, if not wariness. "i think that i'm happy / i think that i'm blessed," Ani sings as she considers her relationship with her partner and her career. She has braved many risks to feel what she's feeling: "i built my empire / out of car tires and chicken wire / and now i'm queen of my own compost heap / and i'm getting used to the smell." The chorus presents one of the sharpest images of Ani's integrity we have heard: "they can call me crazy if i fail / all the chance i need / is one in a million / and they can call me brilliant / if i succeed / gravity is nothing to me / i'm just gonna get my feet wet / until i drown." This may be a typical Ani stance (that of survival against impossible odds), but it assumes new depths (no pun intended) when the image of the artist "swan diving" into the morass of those opposed to her willingly is used. Abandoning one's self to integrity at any cost sounds beautiful, inspiring.

On *Glass House*, rat-tat-tat drumming pushes the guitars forward on the song's chorus. "trapped in my glass house," Ani sings, "a crowd has been gathering outside since dawn," a vivid metaphor for people who constantly question her, to whom she poses the question in turn: "but before you throw stones at me / tell me, what is your house made of?" There is a touch of ennui here, no longer anger towards the self-appointed custodians of her image and soul: "but for the purpose of this song / let's just say i'm doing fine / i think i'm doing fine."

Independence Day promises more than it delivers with the singer questioning her relationship to a former lover who's returned into her life and admitting that when he left "i stopped eating / ... / i was cramped up / and shitting rivers for weeks / and pretending i was finally free." This all occurs against the background of a 4th of July fireworks show. Ani's old-style anger gives way to an odd, unearned sadness.

Pulse is the longest song on any of Ani's albums and one of the most visually striking. Kafka-esque images of giant insects dominate the song as Ani claims undying love for her lover despite "the sight of you there / beautiful and grotesque / and all the rest of that bug stuff / bluffing your way into my mouth / behind my teeth / reaching for my scars." The fact that the other images are revolting ("that night you leaned over / and threw up into your hair") stands in direct contrast to the chorus: "i would offer you my pulse / i would give you my breath." The music slow cooks its way across the minutes as Scot Fisher's accordion solos fill in the background, creating the sound of a quiet, loving, passionate moment caught in flux. There is no world outside, no harsh reality. Though Ani tries to root everything in a starker universality (that of death, of things lasting only for a hundred years, even of burial plots being nothing but ephemera), the emotion that is love overcomes all. Ani's voice returns, soaring placidly over the undulating drum pattern and the quiet guitar strums. *Pulse* is the most passionate, the most loving song she's written. Jon Hassel's third stream trumpet (flowing solidly in muted fashion) gives the song an ethereal landscape.

UP UP UP UP UP UP
(RBR013-D) 1999

'Tis Of Thee (4:42)   *Everest* (5:15)
Virtue (5:07)   *Up Up Up Up Up Up* (3:21)
Come Away From It (8:22)   *Know Now Then* (4:38)
Jukebox (4:27)   *Trickle Down* (3:51)
Angel Food (5:45)   *Hat Shaped Hat* (12:55)
Angry Anymore (3:27)

For UP UP UP UP UP UP (UPX6), Ani and the two Andys (Stochansky and Gilchrist) found themselves back at The Congress House with some recording occurring at Kingsway in New Orleans. Ani's basic touring unit (which had been expanded to include keyboardist Julie Wolf) were the sole musicians to appear. The album was recorded in the summer of 1998 and mastered in NYC under the supervision of Scott Hull.

From the outset, the album sounds of a piece with LITTLE PLASTIC CASTLE, though the funk underpinnings are a marked change over the protean alt-rock/folk-grunge moves of past albums. The songs have a far greater political edge to them — it seemed to some that Ani had tapped herself out writing "I love him but hate him" songs. Perhaps it was Ani's Utah Phillips influences coming to the fore, perhaps it was a genuine will to cross different ground. Whatever the reason, the album charted well yet failed to convert newcomers to her cause. Critical reception was slightly lukewarm despite the high praise from the usual sources (*Rolling Stone, Village Voice, Spin*).

'Tis Of Thee, a State of Our Union address song, condemns the government for widening the gap between the "haves" and the "have-nots." Stark imagery, almost as if one were watching the nightly news, overpowers the singer as she comments on homelessness, while Talk Show TV numbs the masses into complacency. Small pox blankets serve up little warmth as the singer's teeth, clenched and freezing, paint a picture of a harrowing landscape filled with homelessness and despair: "they caught the last poor man / flying away in a shiny cape / they took him to the station / and they said, boy you should've known better / than to try to escape." Definitely one of Ani's best pure political songs, standing squarely in the folk tradition of Pete Seeger and Woody Guthrie.

The funky electric piano and bass phrasings that kick off *Virtue* signal the return of the love-wary side of Ani. Slurred word-play underscores the narrator's seemingly laconic view of herself playing various 'cat' roles, sitting on his lap, prowling the neighborhood, traveling alone, all the while thinking "virtue is relative at best." No triumph here, no celebration, no sense of outrage, just the odd kind of resignation which began to emerge on LITTLE PLASTIC CASTLE.

In *Come Away From It* Ani begs her lover to "come away from it all," to take a step back from the current state of affairs in order to rekindle the way love was. The slow, passionate music fuels Ani's calmly sad reflection: "are you trying to tell me this world / just isn't beautiful enough."

Memory is compared to a jukebox in the Grammy Award nominated song *Jukebox* as the singer sadly reflects upon her past and present state of affairs. The sadness felt in *Come Away From It* appears again, displacing what used to be anger: "i've got a sadness / that grows up around me like a weed / . . . / as she closes her eyes / and hears the song begin again." "This dance is mine," she repeats to herself three times in the final chorus, leaving with a deep sense of loneliness. These are emotions Ani has seldom explored.

Folk funk riffs punctuate *Angel Food* as Ani plays out a complex metaphor of love making: "if the mattress was a table top / and the bed sheet was a page / we'd be written out / like a couple of question marks." The song somehow arrives at the image of angel food: "come to me ready and rude / bring me angel food / angel food." During the recording, drummer Andy Stochansky used a pocket repeater (a small tape device that repeats sounds over and over) as the lights are turned off accidentally. Keyboardist Julie Wolf asks "What is that?" Ani answers "How the fuck would I know!" It's a purely instinctual song, a rare glimpse into Ani's sly, "dirty ol' funkee" self.

On *Angry Anymore* a banjo(!) and accordion announce Ani's song of reconciliation with her parents, a quiet, slightly upbeat song that presents the evolution of the hard-edged singer into a someone who "can learn like the trees / how to bend / how to sway and say/ / i, i think i understand." The simple, self-deprecating way Ani talks about these feelings recalls the glory songs of her very early years, their sad yet fulfilling tone smacking not of nostalgia, but of peace. It's easily the best song on the album and one fans often cite as their favorite.

Every once in a while, the physical world humbles us, not in a belittling way but in a way that makes us feel awe. On *Everest*, Ani and friend walk into a church (an undertone of them being the only white people there seems evident) at seven o'clock on a Sunday night. The voices sing in soaring fashion, begging the stars not to hide, the sky mirrored by an ocean that shows how beautiful the world can be. At the core of the song is a quiet, placid feeling of discovery and rest (everest). Following the emotional and spiritual achievement of *Angry Anymore*, this song also creates a sense of inner peace: "time is not a thing / that's ours to lose / from the height of the pacific / to the depth of everest."

Up Up Up Up Up Up takes on this spiritual dimension as Ani explores the church image again and sings "up, up, up, up, up, up points the / spire of the steeple / but god's work isn't done by god / it's done by people." At the center of the song is her account of a new way of composing songs: "she's learning the spaces she leaves / have their own things to say / she's trying to sing just enough / so that the air around her moves / and make music like mercy / that gives what it is / and has nothing to prove." A rare insight into Ani DiFranco's creative process, with her new *Angry Anymore* attitude at the fore.

The wistful *Know Now Then* portrays a typical Ani emotion sung with lackadaisical abandon framed by a hard-faux-funk groove. There's a haunted feeling to the riffs as voices float edgily above the guitar and drums, while the singer reflects on an old relationship and recognizes, "i didn't know what i now know, then / yeah, i didn't know what i / know now, then."

The title of *Trickle Down* is an ironic attack on contemporary American economic theory, though the song itself is sung in praise of Ani's home town, the working-class Buffalo where "you cease to smell the steel plant / after you've lived here for a while." Ani at her folk best as the music takes on menacing underpinnings — never threatening, yet ominous and foreboding.

Hat Shaped Hat offers more exercises in funkdom from the band as Ani pushes language for effect: 'i said, you are what you do in order to / prevent becoming what you're busy not doing." The band breaks down after eight minutes of fried funk and Ani repeats the lyrics like a mantra, her voice broken, tired, spent. A fake fade out allows the band

and vocalist to return in menacing form as dubbed echo effects crash out the end.

TO THE TEETH
(RBR017-D) 1999

To The Teeth (7:42)	Swing (6:10)
Soft Shoulder (6:04)	Carry You Around (3:24)
Wish I May (4:53)	Cloud Blood (4:51)
Freakshow (5:42)	The Arrivals Gate (4:35)
Going Once (5:33)	Providence (7:18)
Hello, Birmingham (5:23)	I Know This Bar (5:31)
Back, Back, Back (4:46)	

The song lyrics on TO THE TEETH reveal Ani's continuing growth into the calmer emotional and higher spiritual state that characterized UP, UP, UP, UP, UP, UP. Ani again writes lyrics filled with power, grace, vivid imagery, and righteous fire, where the day-to-day musings of a single person give way to the thoughts of a mature, intelligent, aware individual. Ani's had a good number of years to absorb the world around her. At age twenty-nine, the individual sees things in a light far different than when they were nineteen. Add to that a person who is well read, widely traveled, and passionate about her politics, and you have all the right ingredients. Reading the words to Hello Birmingham, for example, filled me with Ani's passion, allowed me to see a side of her that went beyond the L'il Folksinger's usual topic. As with the best of her politically charged songs, many appearing on TO THE TEETH bear the mark of a singer-songwriter in step with today's headlines. For me, it was refreshing.

In a sense, TO THE TEETH is a record driven by yin-yang emotions. Funk and soul music (thanks to a killer, feel-good groove) contrast with anguished lyrics. And though the album may not feature the acoustic side of Ani's craft, her observations remain poignant and passionate.

The cover of TO THE TEETH is almost pitch black, save for the light of a loft window, while the title appears in unfocussed lower case red letters. The album was recorded in three locations: The Dust Bowl in Buffalo (Ani's own studio), Kingsway in New Orleans, and Congress House in Austin, Texas. Ace studio engineer Greg Calbi mastered the album at Sterling Sound in New York, while Ethan Allen provided engineering assistance at Kingsway. Guest musicians include The Artist, Kurt Swinghammer, Maceo Parker, Brian Wolf, Irvin Mayfield, Mark Mullins, and Corey Harper.

Quiet acoustic strumming kicks things off on *To The Teeth*, the album's title track. Ani's sad, low voice tackles an issue ripped out of today's headlines — guns. Guns as used by children who deal with their anguish through violence. Guns as lobbied by the NRA in Washington. Guns in a nation that agrees that these shooting tragedies are unspeakable but has no idea how to stop them. The song can't help but force the listener to remember the senseless shootings in Fort Worth, at Columbine High, in Taber, Alberta . . . and elsewhere. A bass guitar and slight atmospherics underpin Ani's advice on how to solve it all: "open fire on hollywood / open fire on MTV / open fire on NBC / and CBS and ABC." The song ends with the band kicking things into a slow groove (including tuba and trumpet phrasings) as Ani's words of rage sink in: "and if i hear one more time / about a fool's right / to his tools of rage / i'm gonna take all my friends / and i'm gonna move to Canada / and we're gonna die of old age."

Soft Shoulder wastes no time in setting mood and atmosphere thanks to jagged guitar lines, funkified organ fills, and pounding drums. It's slow-burn funk rolls (accented at the end by Maceo Parker's flute) add a sense of nostalgia to a sad song about two people who once knew each other intimately and still carry their affection, regardless of where they are in space and time, underscored by the image of open skies and the highway's soft shoulders.

Kurt Swinghammer's guitar wail ends *Soft Shoulder* and also serves as beginning for *Wish I May*. Lyrically, the song is a lament for empowerment, a call to not fall into "wishing" on stars for righteousness. In a frayed voice that sounds tired and frustrated, Ani states that optimism won't fly in the face of her feelings. As on *Soft Shoulder*, the music is slightly tricked up folk-funk anchored by Jason Mercer's bass. The song ends with soaring choral flights, a direct contrast to the song's lyrical despair.

On *Freakshow*, the listener immediately confronts a turmoil of electric/electronic sounds sung in a carnival-gone-haywire voice that betrays Ani's love for rap and soul. At the core of the song is Ani's sharp acoustic guitar work. The production is superb, allowing the varying elements full room. First listens of the song invariably lead to confusion. Repeated plays show a song rich with life-is-a-carnival imagery and deft performances, both acoustic and electric.

Night sounds (crickets, car wheels on an open road) set the tone for *Going Once*. Irvin Mayfield's twisted trumpet adds an element of the unexpected, while a clavinet and a trombone keep the funk alive. Another song about departures.

Hello Birmingham is a superbly written song about many things — the way Pro-Choice and Pro-Life forces clash in the abortion debate, the assassination of doctors for their beliefs at the hands of extremists who deem their viewpoint as the word of God, the way one part of the world is very much like another when ideologies override thought and logic — all framed within the context of another Election Day. The performances are subtle and understated, while Ani's voice sounds somehow detached, as if she's too close to the topic and chose some distance as she describes the death of Buffalo abortion clinic doctor Albert Slepian. It's a deeply moving, personal performance cast in personal shades. Easily, one of her finest moments on record.

Back Back Back features more trumpet and saxophone on a telegraphed lyric about stepping back from what's going on and taking a good look at the world around you. The funk groove stays true and steady.

Swing kicks things off with a sustained groove and a little slack-keyed guitar. Turntable scratching, vocal dialogue in the background, and a closing rap give the song a modern feel. Both *Swing* and *Back Back Back* sound great if remaining a little vague lyrically.

Experimentation is at the core of *Carry You Around*, another slice-of-thought lyric surrounded by Ani playing drums, keyboards, guitar, and bass, with the voice delivering the words in percussive fashion.

Cloud Blood starts with simple strums of Ani's guitar, but soon the drums add rhythm and Ani's voice sounds muted and jagged as she remembers the act of leaving the one she loved behind. It's all familiar territory framed with slight reggae grooves and road-map imagery.

Again, Kurt Swinghammer's guitar acts as a bridge between *Cloud Blood* and *The Arrivals Gate*. Soon, electronics give way to treated guitar and banjo runs underpinning a wonderfully inventive lyric about the sights and sounds at an airport's arrivals gate. Ani is in particularly fine fashion on a joyful song. The electronically charged percussion and the banjo accent give the song depth and compassion. Even a stream-of-consciousness bridge cannot diminish the power of the melody and the vision of the wordplay. It's the most upbeat moment on the album.

Providence, another in a long line of songs about analyzing why things went wrong and how they can never be the same again, is underscored by quiet music and gospel-like backing vocals. But it's an illusion that lasts only as long as the next verse where sharp, percussive jabs force the pain of the remembrance into sharper focus. The singer realizes the futility of trying to get it all back together again. It is this realization, as reinforced by the chorus' attacks, that gives the song its power and passion. The Artist adds unobtrusive backing vocals.

I Know This Bar also serves up memories. Of a local bar. Of youth lost. Of knowing a place so well it becomes a reason for leaving. It's a sad, downbeat memory, especially given the high funk riffage of earlier songs. A scratchy record sound effect is added to the song's atmosphere towards the end, again underpinning the memories and framing them in the lost language of endings. What could sound more final than the sound of a turntable needle hitting the end-groove repeatedly? Where Ani will begin again on her next album remains a mystery as she continues to grow as a singer-songwriter.

FELLOW WORKERS

THE PAST DIDN'T GO ANYWHERE (with Utah Phillips)
(RBR009-D) 1996

Bridges (8:00)	*Enormously Wealthy* (0:43)
Nevada City, California (6:41)	*Mess With People* (6:43)
Korea (8:31)	*Natural Resources* (2:30)
Anarchy (6:27)	*Heroes* (1:08)
Candidacy (1:45)	*Half A Ghost Town* (4:21)
Bum On The Rod (4:17)	*Holding On* (6:12)

FELLOW WORKERS (with Utah Phillips)
(RBR015-D) 1999

Joe Hill [Instrumental] (2:34)	Why Come? (6:05)
Stupid's Song (2:43)	Unless You Are Free (0:22)
The Most Dangerous Woman (3:43)	I Will Not Obey (2:01)
Stupid's Pledge (0:14)	The Long Memory (5:33)
Direct Action (4:52)	The Silence That Is Me (0:42)
Pie In The Sky (3:30)	Joe Hill (1:37)
Shoot Or Stab Them (2:44)	The Saw-Playing Musician (4:43)
Lawrence (3:29)	Dump The Bosses (1:15)
Bread And Roses (1:45)	The Internationale (2:46)

Fans looking for more angst-ridden female-perspective folk-punk rants from Ani's pen may be put off (at first) by Ani's two releases with folk-singer/activist/legend-in-his-lifetime Utah Phillips. Phillips had released recordings under his own name prior to THE PAST DIDN'T GO ANYWHERE and FELLOW WORKERS releases (some on Philo / Rounder and Alcazar). Known for his pro-union stance and his tales of America's labor force at the turn of the century, his warm voice, charming personality, and dead-pan (though highly sardonic) voice seem a sharp contrast to the slightly mechanical, slow hip-hop grooves Ani builds into the stories on THE PAST DIDN'T GO ANYWHERE.

Ani's liner notes to this album bear repeating to suggest the process Ani went through putting this project together:

"so i sez, i sez, utah, i wanna make an album with you and you don't have to do nothin', i promise. you don't gotta go into some sterile, solitary recording studio and conjure up inspiration on cue. just send me every live recording of yourself that you have lying around and give me your blessing to mess with um. so he says, sure, ok, and compiles a collection of one-of-a-kind cassette recordings representing a smattering of his live performances. then he puts them into a little box and entrusts them to the U.S. postal service. miraculously, thankfully, they arrive at RBR headquarters safely and I had them all transferred to DAT.

"with the tapes de-noised and duped i then embarked on a long solo drive to the congress house in austin, with a trunk full of instruments and a front seat strewn with cassettes. i listened to utah for three days at

75 mph, alternately laughing, weeping, and jotting down cryptic notes on napkins while swerving lane to lane.

"soon as i hit the studio in texas i was setting up rhythm tracks, flying utah's voice around and improvising musically. hardest part was the editing. the way i see it, utah has so much to say that this album coulda easily been two weeks long

"i recorded and mixed the album in 3 weeks and was back in my car for the caffeinated and contemplative drive home. and that's basically the deal. except may for the fact that i think utah is the shit and i loved working on this record, enjoyed it more than any of my own damn records, actually. meditating on the rhythms of his speechsculpting stories into songsmeddling with the work of an american legendsome gall i've got, huh?"

The concept of underscoring spoken word to music using the voice as a "loop" stretches back into the 1940s with the work of American *musique concrete* conductor John Cage and on into the modern era with projects from former Talking Heads guru David Byrne (on MY LIFE IN THE BUSH OF GHOSTS with former Roxy Music synthetist Eno) and performance artist Laurie Anderson. But what was different about Ani's first Utah Phillips collaboration was its sense of completeness. The stories aren't merely sound bites which act as melodic counterpoint. They're the re-contextualization of experiences and thoughts in a vernacular that creates an arch between the time he talks about and the modern era. Much to Ani's credit, she leaves the words intact (for the most part), rarely creating a "dub" styled effect over his voice. But the music is strongly muscular, protean, rhythmically tense (like the clack-clack of the cover art train as it crosses the night).

The collaboration is striking, bold, inventive, and full of intensity and a certain, sad, deprecating humor. Phillips is in fine voice, the warm, comforting tones of his announcer-styled pipes a sharp contrast to his words and images of an America where big government and big business don't give a shit about the state of the common man. His stories reverberate with honesty and a sense of melancholy. Each person recounted in the stories is a genuine hero or heroine, if only because they remained true to their lives, no matter how tragic or wonderful, unfulfilled or lived to the max.

Two other sound bites are added to Utah's stories, segments of speeches by the Reverend Jesse Jackson on "Anarchy" and General Douglas MacArthur on "Korea". These snippets don't rightfully detract from the proceedings so much as they help underpin Phillips' observations (as if they needed further enhancement). Ani performs virtually all the music heard (the lone exception being Darcie Deaville's fiddle on *Nevada City, California*. And can be heard faintly vocalizing on most of the tracks, though more directly on *Holding On*.

For FELLOW WORKERS, a live, in-studio setting was created featuring an 'audience', the musicians , Utah Phillips, and his son. The album was recorded at Kingsway Studios on New Orleans (now a DiFranco favorite). Musicians for the session, billed as Utah's Mensabilly Band, included Ani (on vocals, acoustic, tenor, baritone and steel guitars, banjo, mandolin, thumb piano, and percussion), Julie Wolf (on keyboards, melodica, accordion, and vocals), Jason Mercer (on bass electric and upright, banjo, percussion, and vocals), Daren Hahn (drums, percussion, vocals), Andy Gilchrist (vocals on *Pie In The Sky*), Ethan Allen (vocals on *Dump The Bosses*), and Soul Asylum's Dave Pirner (trumpet on *The Long Memory*). The live feel creates a different environment for Utah's stories. Here, they achieve a far more personal and direct feeling, their power and imagery fully realized by circumstance and atmosphere. While there are no sound bites on FELLOW WORKERS, the album boasts a warm, campfire-sing-along feel that carries bite and power. Of the two releases, FELLOW WORKERS is the more potent and striking. Contributing notes by known historian Howard Zinn (author of *A People's History of the United States*) add insight and awareness without didacticism.

THE SOUNDTRACK

Since 1996, Ani DiFranco has contributed tracks to various television and film projects. Soundtrack appearances have featured, for the most part, songs from Ani's commercially available releases or live versions of songs currently available.

Of her two television appearances on NBC's *Late Night with Conan O'Brien*, one (her performance of *Shameless*) made it on to PolyGram's

1997 soundtrack album LIVE FROM 6A: GREAT MUSICAL PERFORMANCES FROM LATE NITE WITH CONAN O'BRIEN, and she appears on *She's The One* (the soundtrack music was done by eighties rockers Tom Petty & The Heartbreakers). Other TV appearances include *L.A. Doctors, Party Of Five, Slaves To The Underground*, and *Somewhere In The City*, but these aren't available on disc, nor are they likely to be.

Along with contributing a remake of Dusty Springfield's *Wishin' and Hopin'* on MY BEST FRIEND'S WEDDING (Columbia, 1998), Ani acted as the soundtrack co-producer for that movie. And while Ani herself doesn't appear on the *Zero Effect* soundtrack, she does act as the producer for the recording done her good buddy Dan Bern. *Shy* is included on ALL OVER ME/TV (1997) with Ani again acting as producer. She contributed *Million You Never Made* to THE HANGING GARDEN (Virgin, 1997), and on the soundtrack to THE JACKAL (1997), she performs a re-mixed version of *Joyful Girl* (dubbed the *Peace And Love Mix*), but the song does not appear in the movie starring Bruce Willis and Sidney Poitier.

Ani has also appeared on a variety of anthologies for a wide range of causes over the course of time since 1997. Each of these anthologies also features songs previously released or live versions of known numbers. In the case of the Mountain Music series, the albums were created to promote "cult" acts deserving wider recognition.

On AMAZING GRACE (Island Records, 1997), Ani sings *Amazing Grace* as the lead off track to a T. J. Martell benefit album for bone marrow cancer victims. The version here is from DILATE. Ani performs *Buildings And Bridges* live on BEST OF MOUNTAIN STAGE: VOLUME 8 (Oh Boy, 1998) from the famous yearly festival. For DIVINE DIVAS (Rounder, 1997), Ani contributed *Amazing Grace* (same version as on DILATE), an amazing double disc celebration of the world's best female voices. *Fuel* (the same version as on LITTLE PLASTIC CASTLE) is reproduced on FISH TREE BLUES (Bullseye Blues & Jazz, 1999), a benefit album for the Earthjustice Legal Defense Fund (formerly the Sierra Club Legal Defense Fund). For KCRW: RARE ON AIR VOLUME 4 (Mammoth, 1998), Ani performs *Gravel* live on KCRW's airwaves on this ongoing series of albums in support of the National Public Radio station. *Circle of Light* is recorded on LOVE WORTH FIGHTING FOR (Streeter, 1996), while *We're Comin' Up* appears on the SILVERWOLF HOMELESS COMPILATION (Silverwolf, 1995), a benefit for this homeless project. For the Benefit for American Radio Diversity, TELECONNED: WE WANT THE AIRWAVES (No Alternative, 1998), Ani contributed *32 Flavors* in a previously unreleased version.

Ani has contributed to a number of women's recording projects. She sings *Anticipate* on WHAT IS SUMMER MADE FOR (Womad, 1997); *In Or Out* (from IMPERFECTLY) on WOMEN LIKE US: LESBIAN FAVORITES (Rhino, 1997), a benefit for the Lamda Defense & Education Fund; *Egos Like Hairdos* on WOMEN LIVE FROM MOUNTAIN STAGE (Oh Boy, 1996); *Done Wrong* (from DILATE) on WOMEN OF SPIRIT (Putumayo, 1998), with proceeds donated to GROOTS International, a women's resource network; and *Cradle And All* on WOMEN'S WORK (Putumayo, 1996), a live version performed at the Rocky Mountain Folk Festival in benefit of GROOTS. WOMEN IN (E)MOTION (T&M, 1997) is an Ani-produced German radio concert.

For the double disc tribute to the songs of Pete Seeger called WHERE HAVE ALL THE FLOWERS GONE? (Appleseed, 1998), Ani contributes a stunningly graceful and beautiful version of *My Name Is Lisa Kalvelage*. Lisa Kalvelage and two other women tried to stop the shipping of napalm to Vietnam at the height of the Vietnam war in 1965.

Ani has also made guest appearances on albums by other artists. She contributes a cool duet vocal on the ballad *I Love U, But I Don't Trust U Anymore* on The Artist (formerly known as The Artist Formerly Known As Prince)'s latest album, RAVE UN2 THE JOY FANTASTIC (Arista-NPG). For Bruce Cockburn's THE CHARITY OF NIGHT (True North, 1997), she sings backing vocals, as she does on Janis Ian's THE HUNGER (Windham Hill, 1997), adding assorted musical instrumentation and some production to one track. Ani produced Dan Bern's excellent second release, FIFTY EGGS (Work, 1998), and he 'name-drops' her on the song *Chick Singers*.

BLOOD IN THE BOARDROOM

Ani DiFranco appeared on the music scene at a time when the industry was suffering from the malaise of seeing its top '80s sellers wane. The hair bands of the day were no longer selling, and by the start of the 1990s, record companies had abandoned so-called 'modern rock' and were just beginning to get a handle on hard, edgy, grunge music as typified by bands like Mother Love Bone (which later became Pearl Jam), Nirvana, Alice in Chains, Soundgarden. The so-called 'Seattle scene' was beginning to hold court.

As the '90s progressed, the emergence of strong-voiced female singer-songwriters led to a mini-revolution of sorts, culminating in the explosive sales of Alanis Morissette's JAGGED LITTLE PILL. Other record companies began looking for their own Alanis Morissette sound-alike and look-alike. A&R executives tried to sign Ani DiFranco to fill this role only to be rebuked, as we have seen. By 1995 or so, Ani herself had become such an alternative music 'star' that labels began looking for more of her kind to add to their stable of angry young women.

Truth is, the resulting female singer-songwriter movement of the 1990s owed a lot to its pioneers. To the women folk singers of the 1950s and '60s — Ronnie Gilbert (The Weavers), Judy Henske, Carol Hester, Joan Baez, Mimi Farina, and others. The folk movement was the first genre to embrace the feminine perspective. During the late 1960s and '70s, Judy Collins, Odetta, Buffy Ste-Marie, and Joni Mitchell kept the torch burning bright. By the start of the 1970s, more female singer-song-writers made their voices heard — Carole King (whose initial successes had come as a Brill Building songwriter with Neil Sedaka and Lieber-Stoller), Carly Simon, Essra Mohawk, Wendy Waldman, Phoebe Snow, Janis Ian, Laura Nyro (whose evocative songs had provided hits for Three Dog Night), and Patti Smith. With the advent of New Wave rock in the late 1970s and early 1980s, style/image artists found new voice: Lene Lovich, Nina Hagen, Cyndi Lauper. All these women served as a kind of blueprint for the "movement" that emerged in the mid-to-late 1990s.

What emerges below is a list, by no means complete, by no means representative, of the best recordings by Ani's forerunners and contemporaries. These artists (for the most part) operate within the same acoustic alterna-folk-rock-pop setting as Ani. Like Ani, their music is accentuated by intense, passionate, emotional word-play and music that can be quiet, introspective, and withdrawn in one minute, furious, wailing, and harrowing the next. Taken together, these artists have produced a lasting body of music revered for its frankness and strength. Their music, at the very least, speaks from the heart and soars with the soul of lyrical poetry that goes far beyond mere categorizing or pigeon-holing. And the older names appearing here create a vital link with the past. What becomes clear when Ani's work is placed in this context is that she is not the only voice of her generation, though certainly one of the most influential, and that other artists have been both influenced by Ani and have influenced Ani herself.

Tori Amos

BOYS FOR PELE (Atlantic)

LITTLE EARTHQUAKES (EastWest)

UNDER THE PINK (Atlantic)

Laurie Anderson

MISTER HEARTBREAK (Warner Bros.)

Laura Andreone

ALCHEMY (RCA)

Anouk

TOGETHER ALONE (COLUMBIA)

Fiona Apple

TIDAL (WORK)

WHEN THE PAWN . . . (WORK)

Jann Arden

HAPPY? (A&M)

LIVING UNDER JUNE (A&M)

TIME FOR MERCY (A&M)

Joan Armatrading

JOAN ARMATRADING (A&M)

SHOW SOME EMOTION (A&M)

THE KEY (A&M)

THE SHOUTING STAGE (A&M)

WHAT'S INSIDE? (RCA VICTOR)

Bif Naked

BIF NAKED (AQUARIUS)

I BIFICUS (AQUARIUS/ATLANTIC)

Bjork
POST (ELEKTRA)
HOMOGENIC (ELEKTRA)
DEBUT (ELEKTRA)
TELEGRAM (ELEKTRA)

Tracy Bonham
THE BURDENS OF BEING UPRIGHT (ISLAND)

Meredith Brooks
BLURRING THE EDGES (CAPITOL)
DECONSTRUCTION (CAPITOL)

Kate Bush
THE SENSUAL WORLD (COLUMBIA)
THE RED SHOES (COLUMBIA)
THE WHOLE STORY (EMI)

Meryn Cadell
BOMBAZINE (WARNER BROS.)

Mary Chapin Carpenter
PARTY DOLL AND OTHER FAVORITES (COLUMBIA)

Lori Carson
EVERYTHING I TOUCH RUNS WILD (RESTLESS)

Rosanne Cash
KING'S RECORD SHOP (COLUMBIA)
THE WHEEL (COLUMBIA)
10 SONG DEMO (CAPITOL)

Exene Cervenka
OLD WIVES' TALES (RHINO)

Tracy Chapman
TRACY CHAPMAN (ELEKTRA)
CROSSROADS (ELEKTRA)
MATTERS OF THE HEART (ELEKTRA)
NEW BEGINNING (ELEKTRA)

Tony Childs
UNION (A&M)
HOUSE OF HOPE (A&M)
THE WOMAN'S BOAT (DGC)

Paula Cole
HARBINGER (IMAGO/WB)
THIS FIRE (IMAGO/REPRISE)
AMEN (IMAGO/WB)

Shawn Colvin
A FEW SMALL REPAIRS (COLUMBIA)
STEADY ON (COLUMBIA)

Kacy Crowley
ANCHORLESS (ATLANTIC)

(Lisa) Dalbello
WHOMANFORSAYS (CAPITOL)
WHORE (CAPITOL)
SHE (CAPITOL)

Melanie Doane
ADAM'S RIB (COLUMBIA)

Julie Doiron
LONELIEST IN THE MORNING (SUB POP)

Tanya Donnelly
LOVESONGS FOR UNDERDOGS (SIRE)

Melissa Etheridge
MELISSA ETHERIDGE (ISLAND)
BRAVE AND CRAZY (ISLAND)
YES I AM (ISLAND)
NEVER ENOUGH (ISLAND)
YOUR LITTLE SECRET (ISLAND)
BREAKDOWN (ISLAND)

Marianne Faithfull
A PERFECT STRANGER: AN ANTHOLOGY (ISLAND)

Melissa Ferrick
MASSIVE BLUR (ATLANTIC)
WILLING TO WAIT (ATLANTIC)

Nanci Griffith
LAST OF THE TRUE BELIEVERS (ROUNDER)

Emm Gryner
PUBLIC (A&M)
SCIENCE FAIR (DEAD DAISY)

PJ Harvey
RID OF ME (ISLAND)
DRY (ISLAND)
IS THIS DESIRE? (ISLAND)
TO BRING YOU MY LOVE (ISLAND)

Kristen Hersh
HIPS & MAKERS (SIRE)
STRANGE ANGELS (RYKODISC)
SKY MOTEL (RYKODISC)

Hole
LIVE THROUGH THIS (DGC)
CELEBRITY SKIN (DGC)

Penelope Houston
CUT YOU (REPRISE)
TONGUE (REPRISE)

Janis Ian
HUNGER (WINDHAM HILL)

Indigo Girls
INDIGO GIRLS (EPIC)
STRANGE FIRE (EPIC)
NOMADS*INDIANS*SAINTS (EPIC)
COME ON NOW SOCIAL (EPIC)

Kate Jacobs
HYDRANGEA (BAR/NONE)

Jewel (Kilcher)
PIECES OF YOU (ATLANTIC)
SPIRIT (ATLANTIC)

Marti Jones
UNSOPHISTICATED TIME (A&M)
USED GUITAR (A&M)
MY LONGHAIRED LIFE (SUGAR HILL)
LIVE AT SPIRIT SQUARE (SUGAR HILL)

Carole King
TAPESTRY (ODE/EPIC)

Chantal Kreviazuk
UNDER THESE ROCKS AND STONES (COLUMBIA)
COLOUR MOVING AND STILL (COLUMBIA)

Michelle Lewis
LITTLE LEVIATHAN (GIANT)

Suzanne Little
BE HERE NOW (NETTWERK)

Lisa Loeb
TAILS (DGC)
FIRECRACKER (DGC)

Mary Lou Lord
Got No Shadow (Work)

Inger Lorre
TRANSCENDENTAL MEDICATION (TRIPLE X)

Tara MacLean
SILENCE (NETTWERK)

Dayna Manning
VOLUME 1 (EMI)

Amanda Marshal
AMANDA MARSHALL (EPIC)
TUESDAY'S CHILD (EPIC)

Kate & Anne McGarrigle
DANCER WITH BRUISED KNEES (HANNIBAL)
KATE & ANNE MCGARRIGLE (HANNIBAL)
THE FRENCH RECORD (HANNIBAL)
LOVE OVER AND OVER (POLYDOR)
HEARTBEATS ACCELERATING (PRIVATE MUSIC)

Matapedia (Hannibal)
THE MCGARRIGLE FAMILY HOUR (HANNIBAL)

Sarah McLachlan
FUMBLING TOWARDS ECSTASY (ARISTA/NETTWERK)
SURFACING (ARISTA/NETTWERK)
MIRRORBALL (ARISTA/NETTWERK)

Holly McNarland
STUFF (UNIVERSAL)

Natalie Merchant
OPHELIA (ELEKTRA)
TIGER LILY (ELEKTRA)

Joni Mitchell
HITS (REPRISE)
BLUE (REPRISE)
TURBULENT INDIGO (REPRISE)
HEJIRA (ELEKETRA)
LADIES OF THE CANYON (REPRISE)
CLOUDS (REPRISE)
TAMING THE TIGER (REPRISE)

Abra Moore
STRANGEST PLACES (ARISTA)

Mae Moore
OCEANVIEW MOTEL (EPIC)
DRAGONFLY (EPIC)
BOHEMIA (EPIC)

Alanis Morissette
JAGGED LITTLE PILL (MAVERICK)
SUPPOSED FORMER INFATUATION JUNKIE (MAVERICK)

Me'shell Ndegeocello
PLANTATION LULLABIES (MAVERICK)
PEACE BEYOND PASSION (MAVERICK)
BITTER (MAVERICK)

Heather Nova
BLOW (WORK)
OYSTER (WORK)

Laura Nyro
STONED SOUL PICNIC: AN ANTHOLOGY (COLUMBIA)

Sinead O'Connor
THE BEST OF SINEAD O'CONNOR (CHRYSALIS)

Mary Margaret O'Hara
MISS AMERICA (VIRGIN CANADA)

Beth Orton
CENTRAL RESERVATION (ARISTA)
TRAILER PARK (ARISTA)

Joan Osborne
RELISH (BLUE GORILLA/MERCURY)

Linda Perry
IN FLIGHT (INTERSCOPE)

Liz Phair
EXILE IN GUYVILLE (MATADOR)
WHIP-SMART (MATADOR)
WHITECHOCOLATESPACEGG (MATADOR)

Sam Phillips
ZERO ZERO ZERO (VIRGIN)

Phranc
I ENJOY BEING A GIRL (ISLAND)

Poe
HELLO (MODERN)

Eddi Reader
ANGELS & ELECTRICITY (COMPASS)
CANDYFLOSS & MEDICINE (ATLANTIC)
MIRMAMA (COMPASS)

Amy Rigby
DIARY OF A MOD HOUSEWIFE (KOCH)
MIDDLESCENCE (KOCH)

Patti Rothberg
BETWEEN THE 1 AND THE 9 (CAPITOL)

Peggy Seeger
PERIOD PIECES (RYKODISC)

Michelle Shocked
ANTHOLOGY (MERCURY)

Patti Smith
HORSES (ARISTA)
RADIO ETHIOPIA (ARISTA)
EASTER (ARISTA)
WAVE (ARISTA)
DREAM OF LIFE (ARISTA)
GONE AGAIN (ARISTA)
PEACE & NOISE (ARISTA)

Jill Sobule
THINGS HERE ARE DIFFERENT (MCA)
JILL SOBULE (LAVA/ATLANTIC)
HAPPY TOWN (LAVA/ATLANTIC)

Tribe 8
FIST CITY (ALTERNATIVE TENTACLES)
SNARKISM (ALTERNATIVE TENTACLES)
ROLE MODELS FOR AMERIKA (ALTERNATIVE TENTACLES)

Jennifer Trynin
COCKAMAMIE (LAVA)

Suzanne Vega
TRIED AND TRUE: THE BEST OF (A&M)
SUZANNE VEGA (A&M)

Gillian Welch
HELL AMONG THE YEARLINGS (ALMO SOUNDS)
REVIVAL (ALMO SOUNDS)

Susan Werner
TIME BETWEEN TRAINS (BOTTOM LINE)

Lucinda Williams
LUCINDA WILLIAMS (KOCH)
SWEET OLD WORLD (CHAMELEON-ELEKTRA)
CAR WHEELS ON A GRAVEL ROAD (MERCURY)

Victoria Williams
SWING THE STATUE (MAMMOTH)
HAPPY COME HOME (GEFFEN)
LOOSE (MAMMOTH)
MUSINGS OF A CREEKDIPPER (ATLANTIC)

Ani with her fellow worker, Utah Phillips.

Ani DiFranco's art of
album cover and sleeve design.

Lyrics from LIKE I SAID in
Ani's signature handwriting.

**14.
talk to
me now**

he said, ani
you've gotten
tough
because my
tone was curt
yeah, and when
i'm approached
in a dark alley
i don't lift
my skirt
in this city
self preservation
is a full-time
occupation
i'm determined
to survive
on these shores
i don't avert
my eyes
anymore.

**15.
the slant**

the slant
a building settling
around me my
figure female
framed crookedly
in the threshold
of the room
door scraping four
boards with every opening
carving a rough history
of bedroom scenes
the plot
hard to follow
the text
obscured
in the folds of sheets
slowly gathering the stains
of seasons
spent lying there
red and brown
like leaves fallen
the colors
of an eternal cycle
fading with the
wash cycle
and the rinse cycle
again an un-
familiar smell
like my name misspelled
or misspoken
a cycle broken

the sound
of them strong
stalking talking
about their prey

like the wall
hammer meets nail
pounding
they say
pounding
at the rhythms
of attraction
like a woman
was a drum
like a body
was a weapon
like there was something
more they wanted
than the journey
like it was owed
to them
steel toed they walk
and i'm wondering why
this fear of men
maybe it's cuz i'm hungry
and like a baby
i'm dependant on them
to feed me
am a work in progress
dressed in the fabric
of a world unfolding
offering me intricate
patterns of questions

rhythms that never
come clean
and strengths
that you still
haven't seen
ani - voices, drums,
claves

this album is a
compilation of
songs taken from
the albums

ani difranco
1990
— and —
not so soft
1991

the original
albums are still
available by mail
from
righteous babe
records. inc.
(see mail
order info)

Come Away From It

So, what did I learn in the process of unraveling the facts of Ani DiFranco's life, reading her opinions, and dissecting virtually every word she ever wrote and note she ever played? What did I come away with — what should you come away with in listening to Ani DiFranco?

I must admit I had misgivings about the female folk/angst singer/song-writer thing. I've been listening to music since I was ten, writing about it since I was fifteen, getting paid to evaluate it since I was twenty-nine. At some point along the line, I stored Ani DiFranco in a convenient little box labeled "angry-riot-grrl." My research, however, yielded rewards far greater than what I expected. While I was fond of certain women artists from Ani's generation with a similar ideological stance, I learned to view these women and others not as "unique" voices in the wilderness, but as "recurrent" voices in a cultural tradition. After immersing myself in the music of Ani's forebears and contemporaries, I came away with a greater understanding of why these women sing and what they choose to sing about.

Perhaps somewhat self-righteously, I have always prided myself in hearing more in Tom Robinson's *Glad To Be Gay* than just a song about gay liberation. The right of individuals to be what they want to be, without being denigrated by prejudice or denied by custom — this is the text of songs like *Glad To Be Gay*, whether or not you are gay. When Robinson admitted to being bisexual and married a woman (like Ani admitted to being bi and married a man), I never questioned their commitment to freedom, their sincerity, their passion. As I studied Ani DiFranco, I was

163

able to see these qualities not only in her but also in artists I had previously dismissed. Ani DiFranco came along at a time in popular music history when the roar of rock had been dulled by the slap-thigh-kick-twirl of new country, the blam-blam-blam of life in "da hood" rap, and the alien rites of the rock charts. Some of us, unable to deal with Alice in Chains, Shania Twain, or Tupac Shakur, turned to one of the other sources of honesty left in the music world — to Ani DiFranco, Alanis Morissette, Jewel, Tori Amos, and their colleagues. I learned to appreciate the wry humor of Jill Sobule and saw so much of Ani DiFranco there, especially on Jill's infamous "hit" *I Kissed A Girl*, the sad abandon of Beth Orton's *Couldn't Cause Me Harm*, the brutal honesty of Liz Phair's *Fuck And Run*. For some reason, very few men were willing or able to reveal so much of themselves in such brutal, honest fashion. Ani's intense words and no-nonsense, angular, jagged music all reminded me that living in this world may not be such a big deal, but staying true to one's ideals, no matter what the pitfalls or rewards may be, is. And ultimately, far more satisfying.

Ani DiFranco's sense of adventure, undertaking a journey, unplanned, traveling an uncharted course, fascinated me. As her fame spread, the degree to which she retained control over her life and art should have (logically) declined, as is the case for most recording artists. In the face of various temptations, derision, and detraction, Ani DiFranco maintained control. We all exercise control over our lives and our livelihoods in some degree, but most of us submit to temptations of reward of some kind or other from a corporate society eager to own us. Ani DiFranco has faced the same temptation but has kept her values intact, regardless of what the world has thrown at her to dislodge her convictions, regardless of what the world has offered her in order to submit.

But what I came away with that surpasses these cultural, moral, and political lessons is a deeper appreciation for Ani DiFranco's music. To abandon yourself to her music goes beyond the pleasures of knowledge into a world of joy. Ani DiFranco may deny being an angry girl or a pretty girl, but her music comes from the heart and soul of a joyful girl.

References

Ali, Lorraine. Untitled. *US Magazine*, December 1996.

Anonymous. "Ani's Alternative Success." *www.cnnfn.com*. November 22, 1996.

_____. "Ani DiFranco." *www.mtv.com/news/difranco*.

_____. "Ani DiFranco." *www.allmusic.com*.

_____. "Ani Difranco ... My Name Is Lisa Kalvelage." *www.appleseedrec.com*.

_____. "Ani Interview." *Sessions at West 54th. www.imperfectly.com/ani*.

_____. "Quotes." *www.members.tripod.com*.

Apter, Jeff. "Ani DiFranco Putting Finishing Touches ...." *Rocktropolis Allstar News*, February 1998.

Avery, D.M. "Living in Clip." *CMJ: New Music Report*, May 5, 1997.

Bell, Carrie. "Righteous Babe's DiFranco Moves 'Up'." *Billboard*, November 28, 1998.

Byrkit, Becky. "Up Up Up Up Up Up." *www.allmusic.com*.

Cherkis, Jason. "The New Folk Renegades." *Option Magazine*, May-June 1994.

Chonin, Neva. "DiFranco Raises the Volume: Punk-Folk Icon Grows into Rock Star." *San Francisco Chronicle*, June 27, 1998.

DiFranco, Ani. "Court and Spark." *Los Angeles Times Magazine*, September 20, 1998.

Dougherty, Steve. "Up Up Up Up Up Up." *People Weekly*, January 25, 1999.

Ehmke, Ron (The Righteous Babe Records Minister of Communications) "An Open Letter from Ani DiFranco." *www.columbia.edu*.

Eliscu, Jenny. "I Am Not a Pretty Girl." *CMJ: New Music Report*, July 3, 1995.

Erlewine, Michael, et al, eds. *All Music Guide*. 2nd ed. New York: Miller Freeman, 1994.

Frampton, Megan. "Dilate." *CMJ: New Music Report*, May 27, 1996.

Frampton, Scott. "Ani DiFranco: Do the Evolution." *CMJ: New Music Report*, February 1999.

Hughes, Kim. "Little Plastic Castle." *Now Magazine*, February 1998.

Jackson, Alan. "Woman on the Edge of a Breakthrough." *London Times*, February 1998.

Kelp, Larry. "Pop Quiz — Q&A with Ani DiFranco." *San Francisco Chronicle*, November 12, 1995.

Larkin, Colin. *Virgin Encyclopedia of Indie & New Wave*. London: Virgin, 1998.

Lloyd, Emily. "Ani DiFranco Has Lots of Luck with Girls." *Off Our Backs*, November 1994.

McLaughlin, Megan. "Out of Range." *CMJ: New Music Report*, June 20, 1994.

Mechanic, Michael. "Interview with Ani DiFranco." *Mother Jones*, September 8, 1999.

Michel, Sia. "Folk Implosion." *Spin Magazine*, October 1996.

Morse, Steve. "Like Her Label, DiFranco Aims To Be 'Righteous Babe'." *The Boston Globe*, June 6, 1998.

Newman, Jeffrey L. "Queer Girl from Buffalo." *Hero Magazine*, 1999.

Newman, Melinda. "DiFranco's Righteous Babe Label Taking on Other Acts." *Billboard*, July 3, 1999.

O'Brien, Lucy. "Power Babe." *Diva*, February/March 1998.

Obejas, Achy. "Both Sides Now." *The Advocate*, December 9, 1997.

Papazian, Ellen. "Ani DiFranco Is the Hottest Indie Musician around and an Icon for Her Generation — But at What Price?" *Ms.*, November 1996.

Perlich, Tim. "Up Up Up Up Up Up." *Now Magazine*, March 1999.

Reiss, Al. "Ani DiFranco: The Tazmanian Devil of Folk." *Dirty Linen*, October-November 1994.

Revkin, Andrew C. "How a Righteous Babe Saved Her Hometown." *The New York Times*, February 16, 1998.

Righteous Babe Records. "Righteous Babe Records Studykit: Ani DiFranco: Biography." Updated 2/4/98. *www.anidifranco.org*.

_____. "Righteous Babe Records Studykit: Righteous Babe Story." Updated 2/4/98. *www.anidifranco.org*.

_____. "Ani DiFranco: On Her Own (The Righteous Babe Records Story)." *www.anidifranco.net (Absolute Ani)*.

_____. "Exhibit 015-D-02: U. Phillips Resume."

_____. "Exhibit 015-D-03: Interview Transcript/Ani DiFranco/Utah Phillips."

Robicheau, Paul. "Taking Aim." *The Boston Globe*, May 12, 1994.

Robins, Ira A. *The Trouser Press Guide to 90s Rock.* New York: Fireside, 1997.

Rodgers, Jeffrey Pepper. "Radical Folk." *Acoustic Guitar,* August 1997.

Rotondi, James. "Ani DiFranco's Ferocious Folk." *Guitar Player,* December 1994.

Spera, Keith. Untitled. *The Times-Picayune,* December 11, 1998.

Stinkdog and Venus, "Interview with Ani DiFranco." *Monkey Magnet,* November 1998.

Sullivan, James. "Ani Has the Answer." *San Francisco Chronicle,* November 1997.

Teshima, John. "Ani DiFranco." *Chart Magazine,* 1996.

Tortorici, Frank. "Dylan, DiFranco: The Perfect One-Two Punch." *Addicted to Noise: The On-line Rock & Roll Magazine (www.addict.com).*

Volk, Nicole. "People's Poetry Festival." *Music Blvd,* April 1999.

Woodworth, Marc, ed. *Solo: Women Singer-Songwriters in Their Own Words.* New York: Delta, 1998.

Acknowledgements

The author would like to thank the following people for their assistance with this book. Lynda Quirino, soul-mate extraordinaire, support system, best and worst critic. Tracy Mann, publicist *par excellence*. Bob Hilderley, publisher, for making the suggestion in the first place, allowing it to happen on my own terms, and having the patience to see it through all the way with a writer with "first book" jitters. Peter Sauve, journalist without reserve, moral backbone, and a damn good golfer. The clans Quirino and Kostovchik, who never lost faith despite setbacks and reschedulings. Everyone at Columbia House Canada, for constant understanding. Helen Brodbeck and Sarah Jerrom, for insight and perspective. Special thanks to Sean Powers for his photographs and for creating his "Absolute Ani" web site.

The author and the publisher gratefully acknowledge the following agencies and individuals for images and photographs reproduced in this book. For publicity photographs appearing on p. 2 (by Alex Sanchez) and p. 159 (by Steven Stone), and images from Ani DiFranco press kits on pp. 6 (Righteous Babe Records Catalog 1999), 21 (Ani DiFranco Resume), 96 (L'il Old Ani DiFranco Press Kit Winter 1999), and 100 (Up, Up, Up, Up, Up, Up postcard), Fleming/Tamulevich & Associates and Righteous Babe Records. For photographs and images appearing on pp. 18, 19, 65-72, 97, 98, and the cover, Sean Powers.